# WELCOME

This collection of handmade heirlooms combines the time-honored tradition of quilt making with the treasured art of appliqué.

You'll find refreshing designs for every season, holiday, and gift occasion. You may want to re-create them exactly—or create a color palette for each special project.

The book covers the gamut of appliqué techniques, from traditional hand stitching to fused fabric. It includes projects that are sized for every space—from place mats and table quilts to wall hangings and bed quilts.

"Appliqué Primer" and "Quilting Basics" provide step-by-step instruction on appliqué techniques and quilt making. These sections are especially helpful for beginners—but even seasoned stitchers should review them. Steady progress and stunning results make learning new skills a pleasure—and accomplishing ever more interesting challenges, a delight.

Explore your creativity by adding a little appliqué to your next quilting project—or by using a quilt as the base for your next appliqué project.

You'll see: Handmade heirlooms that combine the arts are simply fun!

Enjoy!

# Appliqué Primer

The time-honored tradition of appliqué—adding fabric motifs to a foundation fabric—allows for freedom in design not always available with piecing. Styles range from simple to intricate, primitive to elegant. Appliqué can be done by hand or machine. Numerous appliqué methods have been developed, giving quiltmakers choices when it comes to the finished appearance.

## Templates

An appliqué template is a pattern used to trace the appliqué shape onto fabric. The template's material depends on how often the template will be used. Make sure that your template will hold up to the wear that it receives from multiple tracings without deteriorating at the edges. A sturdy, durable material such as template plastic, available at quilt and crafts supply stores, is suitable for making permanent templates for scissors-cut appliqué pieces.

### MAKING APPLIQUÉ TEMPLATES

**1.** For most appliqué techniques you need to make your templates the exact size of the finished pieces with no seam allowances included. The seam allowances are added when you cut out the appliqué pieces. Trace the patterns onto template plastic using a permanent marker. Use a ruler for any straight lines.

**2.** Mark each appliqué template with its letter designation, grain line (if indicated), block name, and appliqué sequence order. Mark an X on edges that do not need to be turned under and transfer the Xs to the fabric shapes when you trace around the templates.

**3.** Cut out each template, then verify their accuracy by placing them over their printed patterns.

### USING APPLIQUÉ TEMPLATES

**1.** Choose a marking tool to trace around the templates on fabric. A pencil works well on light-color fabric; a white, silver, or yellow dressmaker's pencil is a good choice on dark-color fabric. If you're using a pencil, keep the point sharp to ensure accuracy. Do not use a ballpoint or ink pen; it may bleed when washed. Test all marking tools on a fabric scrap before using them.

**2.** Place templates on the fabric, positioning them at least ½" apart. (Whether you place them faceup or facedown on the fabric's right or wrong side depends on the appliqué method you choose.) Trace around each template with your selected marking tool. The drawn lines represent the sewing lines. The specific appliqué technique you choose will dictate how much, if any, seam allowance you leave when cutting out the shape.

**3.** Cut out the appliqué shapes, including seam allowances if necessary for your chosen appliqué method.

### STITCHING SEQUENCE

Edges of appliqué pieces that will be covered by other pieces do not need to be turned under before they are appliquéd. By preparing all your appliqué pieces at one time, you can plan any overlaps, which will save stitching time and considerable bulk in the finished project.

If your pattern does not indicate a numerical stitching sequence, observe which piece is closest to the foundation fabric and farthest away from you. That is the first piece you should appliqué to the foundation. Appliqué the rest of the pieces to the foundation, working from the bottom layer to the top.

# Prepare Appliqué Pieces

Prepare your appliqué pieces according to the needs of your chosen appliqué method. Preparation options include basting, freezer paper, spray starch, double appliqué, and fusible web. Read the introduction to each method that follows to determine which one will work for your selected method.

## BASTING METHOD

This method uses a reusable template, marking tool, and thread to prepare appliqué pieces for hand or machine appliqué.

**1.** Place your templates on the right side of the fabric, positioning them at least ½" apart; trace.

**2.** Cut out the appliqué shapes, adding a ³⁄₁₆" seam allowance to all edges. Clip inside curves and points to within a thread of the marked lines, making clips closer together in the curved areas. Try to make your clips on the bias grain of the seam

allowance, which means your clips will be often diagonal, rather than perpendicular, lines. This directional clipping prevents fabric from raveling while you're working with the edges. *Note:* Some hand quilters who use the needle-turn appliqué method choose to stop their appliqué preparation with this step.

**3.** Working from the right side of the appliqué piece and beginning at an inner point, use a contrasting color thread to baste the seam allowance under following the marked lines. For easier removal of the thread later, begin and end your basting thread on the right side of appliqué piece.

**4.** For a sharp outer point, fold the fabric straight over the point.

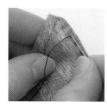

**5.** Then fold in an adjacent seam allowance, overlapping the folded point. Baste in place.

**6.** As you reach the outer point, fold over the remaining adjacent seam allowance and continue basting around the shape.

## USING FREEZER PAPER

Many quilters choose to use freezer paper for appliqué. Available in grocery stores and some quilt shops, freezer paper has a shiny coating on one side that temporarily adheres to fabric when pressed with a warm iron. It is not necessary to consider the grain line of the fabric when utilizing freezer-paper templates.

## FREEZER-PAPER METHOD 1

This method uses freezer-paper templates to hold the seam allowances of the appliqué pieces in place. (Refer to Using Freezer Paper for additional information.) This technique may be used to prepare pieces for hand or machine appliqué.

**1.** Trace the appliqué patterns on the dull side of the freezer paper. Cut out the shapes on the traced lines to make freezer-paper templates.

**2.** Place the freezer-paper templates dull side up on the right side of the fabric. While holding the freezer paper in place, cut the shapes from fabric, adding a ³⁄₁₆" seam allowance to all edges.

**3.** Turn the freezer-paper templates shiny side up and place on the wrong sides of the appliqué shapes. Clip the

# Appliqué Primer

inside curves or points on the appliqué shapes. When clipping inside curves, clip halfway through the seam allowances. Try to make your clips on the bias grain of the seam allowance, which means your clips often will be diagonal, rather than perpendicular, lines. This directional clipping prevents fabric from raveling while you're working with the edges.

**4.** Beginning at an inner point of an appliqué shape, use the tip of a hot, dry iron to push the seam allowance over the edge of the freezer paper. The seam allowance will adhere to the shiny side of the freezer paper. *Note:* Do not touch the iron soleplate to the freezer paper past the turned fabric edge.

**5.** Continue working around the appliqué shape, turning one small area at a time and pressing the seam allowance up and over the freezer paper. Make certain the appliqué fabric is pressed taut against the edges of the freezer-paper template.

Small pleats in the fabric may appear as you round outer curves. If there is too much bulk in a seam allowance, make small V clips around outer curves to ease the fabric around the edge.

**6.** For a sharp outer point, fold the fabric straight over the point of the freezer-paper template; press to freezer paper.

**7.** With the tip of the iron, push an adjacent seam allowance over the edge of the freezer paper. Repeat with the remaining adjacent seam allowance, pushing the seam llowance taut to ensure a sharp point.

**8.** After all edges are pressed, let the appliqué shape cool, then either remove the freezer-paper template before proceeding with the desired hand- or machine-appliqué technique or leave in to stitch.

## FREEZER-PAPER METHOD 2

This technique involves pressing entire freezer-paper templates, shiny side down, to the appliqué fabric. The freezer paper is removed before the appliqué is sewn in place. This technique may be used to prepare pieces for hand or machine appliqué.

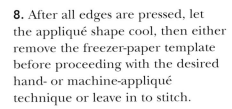

**1.** Trace a reverse image of the appliqué pattern on the dull side of the freezer paper. Cut out the shape on the traced lines to make a freezer-paper template. *Note:* To create a reverse image, tape the appliqué pattern facedown on a light box or sunny window.

**2.** Place the appliqué fabric wrong side up on a pressing surface. With a dry iron on a cotton setting, press a freezer-paper shape, shiny side down, to the appliqué fabric. Leave the iron on the paper for a few seconds. Lift the iron to check that the template is completely adhered to the fabric. If the template is not completely adhered, press again.

**3.** Cut out the appliqué shape, adding a 3/16" seam allowance to all edges. Clip inside curves or points on the appliqué shape. When clipping inside curves, clip halfway through the seam allowances. Try to make your clips on the bias grain of the seam allowance, which means clips often will be diagonal, rather than perpendicular, lines. This directional clipping prevents fabric from raveling while you're working with the edges.

**4.** Beginning at one inner point of an appliqué shape, use the tip of a hot, dry iron to push the seam allowance over the edge of the freezer paper. *Note:* The seam allowance will not adhere to the dull side of the freezer paper.

**5.** Continue working around the appliqué shape, turning one small area at a time and pressing the seam allowance up and over the freezer paper. Make certain the appliqué fabric is pressed taut against the edges of the freezer-paper template.

Small pleats in the fabric may appear as you round outer curves. If there is too much bulk in a seam allowance, make small V clips around outer curves to ease the fabric around the edge.

**6.** For a sharp outer point, fold the fabric straight over the point of the freezer-paper template; press.

**7.** With the tip of the iron, push an adjacent seam allowance over the edge of the freezer paper. Repeat with the remaining adjacent seam allowance, pushing the seam allowance taut to ensure a sharp point.

**8.** After all edges are pressed, let the appliqué shape cool, then remove the freezer-paper template.

## FREEZER-PAPER METHOD 3

This technique involves pressing the shiny side of the freezer-paper templates to the right side of the appliqué fabric. The seam allowances are not turned under. This technique may be used to prepare pieces for needle-turn appliqué.

**1.** Trace a finished-size appliqué pattern onto the dull side of the freezer paper. Cut out the shape on the traced lines to make a freezer-paper template.

**2.** Place the appliqué fabric right side up on a pressing surface. With a dry iron on a cotton setting, press a freezer-paper template, shiny side down, to the appliqué fabric. Leave the iron on the paper for a few seconds. Lift the iron to check that the template is completely adhered to the fabric. If the template is not completely adhered, press again.

**3.** Cut out the appliqué shape, adding a 3⁄16" seam allowance to all edges. Clip inside curves or points on the appliqué shape. When clipping inside curves, clip halfway through the seam allowance. Try to make your clips on the bias grain of the seam allowance, which means your clips often will be diagonal, rather than perpendicular, lines. This directional clipping prevents fabric from raveling while you're working with the edges.

**4.** Do not remove the template until the appliqué piece is stitched in place.

## DOUBLE-APPLIQUÉ METHOD

This method eases the challenge of turning under seam allowances by facing the appliqué pieces with sheer, featherweight, nonfusible, nonwoven interfacing. This technique may be used to prepare pieces for hand or machine appliqué.

**1.** Place a rigid template wrong side up on the wrong side of the appliqué fabric; trace. The traced line is your stitching line.

**2.** With right sides together, layer your appliqué fabric with a like-size piece of sheer, featherweight, nonfusible, nonwoven interfacing.

**3.** Sew the pieces together, stitching on the marked line. Cut out the appliqué shape, adding a 3⁄16" seam allowance to all edges.

# Appliqué Primer

**4.** Trim the interfacing seam allowance slightly smaller than the appliqué fabric. This will enable the seam allowance to roll slightly to the back side of the appliqué once it is turned. Clip at the inner curves and points.

**5.** Clip a small slit in the center of the interfacing, being careful not to cut through the appliqué fabric.

**6.** Turn the appliqué right side out through the slit.

**7.** Press the appliqué piece from the right side.

## FUSIBLE WEB METHOD

Manufacturer's instructions for adhering fusible web vary by brand. Follow the instructions that come with your fusible web to ensure success. Factors such as the iron's temperature setting, a dry or steam iron, and the length of time you press are critical to attaining a secure bond between the fusible web and the fabric.

This method eliminates the need to turn under any seam allowances. Choose a lightweight, paper-backed fusible web that can be stitched

through unless you plan to leave the appliqué edges unfinished. This technique is commonly used for machine appliqué, but also can be used for hand appliqué.

**1.** Position the fusible web with the paper side up over the appliqué pattern and place on a light box. Use a pencil to trace each pattern the specified number of times. If you are tracing multiple pieces at one time, leave at least ½" between tracings. *Note:* If you are not using an appliqué pattern designed especially for fusible web, you will need to create a mirror image of the pattern before tracing it. If you don't, your appliqués will be reversed once you cut them from fabric. To create a reverse image, tape the appliqué pattern facedown on a light box or sunny window.

Cut out the traced appliqué pattern roughly ¼" outside the traced lines. Do not cut directly on the traced lines.

**2.** If you are working with multiple appliqué layers or want to reduce the stiffness of the finished project, consider cutting away the center of your fusible web shapes. To do this, cut ¼" inside the traced lines and discard the centers.

**3.** Place the fusible-web shape paper side up on the back of the designated appliqué fabric.

Press in place following the manufacturer's instructions. Do not slide the iron, but pick it up to move it from one area to the next. Let the appliqué shape cool.

**4.** Cut out the fabric shape on the drawn lines. Peel off the paper backing.

# Make Bias Stems

Fabric strips needed to make curved appliqué stems and vines should be cut on the bias so that they are flexible enough to bend without wrinkles or puckers.

## CUTTING BIAS STRIPS

Strips for curved appliqué pattern pieces, such as meandering vines, and for binding curved edges should be cut on the bias, which runs at a 45° angle to the selvage of a woven fabric and has the most give or stretch.

To cut bias strips, begin with a fabric square or rectangle. Use a large acrylic ruler to square up the left edge of the fabric. Then make a cut at a 45° angle to the left edge (see Bias Strip Diagram). Handle the diagonal edges carefully to avoid distorting the bias. To cut a strip, measure the desired width parallel to the 45° cut edge; cut. Continue cutting enough strips to total the length needed.

Bias Strip Diagram

## BIAS BAR METHOD

This method uses metal or heat-resistant plastic bias bars purchased in a size to match the desired finished width of the bias stem. If instructions for strip width and seam allowance are provided with your bias bars, refer to them. If not, refer to the following.

**1.** Cut a bias strip twice the desired finished width plus ¾". For example, for a ½"-wide finished bias stem, cut a 1¾"-wide bias strip. Handle the strip's edges carefully to prevent stretching. Fold the strip in half lengthwise with the wrong side together; lightly press.

**2.** Stitch the length of the strip with the folded edge on the machine seam guide (to the right of the presser foot), the raw edges to the left, and a seam allowance equivalent to the desired finished width. For example, for a ½"-wide finished bias stem, stitch ½" away from the folded edge.

**3.** Trim away the seam allowance, leaving only enough fabric to hold the seam intact (about ¹⁄₁₆").

**4.** Slide the bias bar into the stem with the seam allowance centered on a flat side of the bar.

Press the seam allowance to one side so that neither the seam nor the seam allowance is visible along the edges.

**5.** Remove the bar from the stem, and press the stem again.

**6.** Trace the stem placement line on the appliqué foundation fabric as a seam guide.

**7.** Pin the bias stem to the appliqué foundation covering the marked line and secure the stem in place using a machine blind hem stitch or slip-stitching by hand.

## FINGER-PRESSING METHOD

**1.** Cut a bias strip to the desired finished width plus ½". For example, for a ¼"-wide finished bias stem, cut a ¾"-wide bias strip. Handle the strip's edges carefully to prevent stretching.

**2.** Finger-press under ¼" along both long edges.

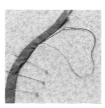

**3.** Pin the bias stem to the appliqué foundation and secure the stem in place using a machine blind hem stitch or slip-stitching by hand.

## Position the Appliqué Pieces

**1.** Cut the appliqué foundation fabric larger than the desired finished size to allow for any take-up in the fabric that might occur during the appliqué process. For example, for a 12" finished square, cut a 14"-square appliqué foundation. When the appliqué is complete, you'll trim the foundation to 12½" square. (The extra ¼" on each side will be used for seam allowances when assembling the quilt top.)

**2.** Fold the square appliqué foundation in half vertically and horizontally to find the center and divide the square into quarters. Lightly finger-press to create positioning guides for the appliqué pieces.

**3.** Then fold the square appliqué foundation diagonally in both directions and lightly finger-press to make additional positioning guidelines.

**4.** Draw corresponding vertical, horizontal, and diagonal positioning guidelines on your full-size appliqué pattern if they are not already marked.

**5.** Prepare the appliqué pieces using the desired method. Referring to your appliqué pattern, pin and stitch the appliqué pieces to the foundation using your desired method; work from the bottom layer up.

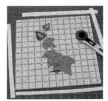

**6.** After the appliqué is complete, trim the appliqué foundation to the desired finished size plus seam allowances.

## Hold Appliqué Pieces in Place

Once the appliqués and foundations have been prepared for stitching, the appliqué pieces can be held in place with pins, basting threads, spray adhesive, fusible web, or fabric glue stick. The number of appliqué layers you are working with may influence your choice.

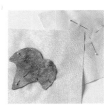

**Pins:** Use as many straight pins as needed to hold each appliqué piece in place on the appliqué foundation for both machine and hand appliqué. Pins are generally used to hold no more than two layers at a time and are pushed through from the top. Some hand appliquérs like to place pins on the back side of the work to prevent catching thread in pins as they work. Remove the pins as you stitch.

**Basting:** Sewing long stitches about ¼" from the turned-under edges is another way to secure prepared appliqué pieces to a foundation for both machine and hand appliqué. Begin and end the basting stitches on the right side of the appliqué for easier removal. You may wish to remove basting stitches when the entire appliqué work is complete or, if the basting threads impede stitching progress, remove them as you go. This is the preferred method of quilters who wish to hold multiple appliqué layers in position at once before permanently stitching them in place.

**Fabric basting spray:** When lightly sprayed on the wrong side of appliqué pieces, this adhesive usually allows you to position and reposition appliqués while you work. It can hold appliqués in place for both machine and hand appliqué. Work in a well-ventilated area and cover your work surface with paper. Be careful to spray lightly, as overspraying can cause a gummy build-up that makes stitching difficult.

**Fabric glue or glue stick:** Apply these adhesives lightly to the wrong side of the prepared appliqué pieces along the outer edges or in the center. Press the appliqué piece to the appliqué foundation fabric. Be sure to apply the glue sparingly to avoid a build-up that would be difficult to stitch through. This method can be used for both machine and hand appliqué.

---

**Tip:** If residue from basting spray or a glue stick builds up on your needle, wipe it off with rubbing alcohol.

---

**Fusible web:** This adhesive is most often used to hold pieces in position for machine appliqué. If you have an appliqué project with multiple layers of pieces that are prepared with fusible web, you may wish to hold them in position before adhering them to the foundation. To do so, place your full-size appliqué pattern beneath a clear, nonstick pressing sheet. Layer the prepared appliqué pieces in position right side up on the pressing sheet. Press lightly, just enough to fuse the pieces together, following the manufacturer's instructions. Do not slide the iron, but pick it up and move it from one area to the next. Let the pieces cool, then remove the fused appliqués from the pressing sheet and fuse them to the appliqué foundation.

## Hand Appliqué

There are many ways to hand-stitch pieces in place on an appliqué foundation. If you're new to hand appliqué, experiment with each to determine which method is most comfortable for you.

For most hand appliqué, use a sharp, between, straw, or milliners needle and the finest thread you can find that matches the appliqué pieces. The higher the number, the finer the thread, so look for silk or fine cotton machine-embroidery threads; they will make your appliqué stitches nearly invisible.

# Traditional Appliqué Stitch

This technique uses appliqué pieces that have had the seam allowances turned under. For best results, use a sharp, between, straw, or milliners needle.

**1.** Prepare the appliqué pieces by turning the seam allowances under. Pin, baste, or glue an appliqué piece in place on the appliqué foundation.

**2.** Working with a length of thread no longer than 18", insert the needle into the wrong side of the appliqué foundation directly beneath the edge of the appliqué piece. Bring the needle up through the rolled edge of the appliqué piece.

Tip: If you're using appliqué pieces that have the freezer-paper template inside the appliqué shape while it's being stitched, be sure your stitching catches the fabric edge only. Keeping the paper template clear of stitching makes it easier to remove once the appliqué is stitched down.

**3.** Hold the needle parallel to the edge of the appliqué with the point of the needle next to the spot where the thread just exited.

**4.** Slide the point of the needle under the appliqué edge, into the appliqué foundation, and forward about ⅛" to ³⁄₁₆", bringing the needle point out through the rolled edge of the appliqué.

**5.** Give the thread a gentle tug to bury the stitch in the fabric and allow the appliqué shape to rise up off the foundation. Continue stitching in the same manner around the shape along rolled edge.

Tip: Match your thread color to the appliqué pieces. *Note:* Contrasting thread was used in the photos for illustration purposes only.

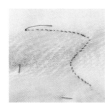
**6.** On the wrong side of the appliqué foundation, the stitches will be slightly angled.

**7.** End the thread by knotting it on the wrong side of the foundation, beneath the appliqué piece.

**8.** Once all pieces have been appliquéd, press the foundation from the wrong side and trim it to the desired size, including the seam allowances.

Tip: Removing a freezer-paper template after an appliqué shape has been stitched in place can be done in a couple of different ways.

- You may stitch the appliquéd shape to the foundation, leaving a small opening to pull out the template. Use the tip of your needle to loosen the freezer-paper template. Pull the template out through the opening and stitch the opening closed.

- You may stitch the entire appliqué shape in place. From the wrong side, carefully snip through the appliqué foundation only. Remove the template through the opening, then stitch the opening closed.

# Needle-Turn Appliqué

This technique involves turning under the appliqué seam allowance as you stitch. For best results, use a straw or milliners needle. The extra length of these needles aids in tucking fabric under before taking stitches.

**1.** Prepare the appliqué pieces following Freezer-Paper Method 3 or by completing steps 1 and 2 of the Basting Method. Pin, baste, or glue an appliqué piece in place on the appliqué foundation.

 **2.** Working with a length of thread no longer than 18", insert the needle into the wrong side of the appliqué foundation directly beneath the edge of the appliqué piece. Bring your needle up between the appliqué and the foundation. Use the point of the needle to sweep the seam allowance under about 1" or so ahead of your stitching and secure the fabric with your thumb. The edge of the freezer-paper template or the drawn line serves as your guide for how much to turn under.

 **3.** Hold the needle parallel to the edge of the appliqué with the needle's point at the spot where the thread just exited. Slide the point of the needle under a thread or two along the appliqué's rolled edge. Give the thread a gentle tug to bury the stitch in the fabric and allow the appliqué shape to rise up off the foundation.

**4.** Then place the tip of the needle into the appliqué foundation and rock it forward, bringing the tip up into the rolled appliqué edge about ⅛" to ³⁄₁₆" away from the previous stitch. Pull the needle through and gently tug the thread to bury the stitch as before.

**5.** Continue in the same manner around the entire appliqué, taking tinier stitches around inside corners and curves where the seam allowances are more scant. Use the needle point to manipulate the seam

allowance to lie flat in outside curves.

**6.** End the thread by knotting it on the wrong side of the foundation, beneath the appliqué piece.

**7.** Once all pieces have been appliquéd, press the foundation from the wrong side and trim it to the desired size, including the seam allowances.

# Machine Appliqué

## BEGINNING AND ENDING STITCHING

 **1.** To begin stitching, bring the bobbin and needle threads to the top; this helps prevent thread tangles and snarls on the wrong side of your work. To begin this way, put the presser foot down and take one stitch. Stop and pull the bobbin thread to the top.

 **2.** Set your machine for a narrow zigzag or satin stitch. Holding the bobbin and needle threads to one side, take a few stitches on a curve or straight edge; do not start at an inner or outer point. (If your machine has a variable stitch length, you may wish to set your stitch length at 0 and take a few stitches, one on top of

the next, to lock threads in place at the start.) Reset your machine to the desired stitch setting; stitch about 1" and trim off the thread tails. Or, when the appliqué work is completed, use a needle to draw the thread tails to the wrong side of the work and bury them in the stitching.

**Tip:** For machine appliqué, use a 60/8, 70/10, 75/11, or 80/12 sharp needle. For best results, use a smaller number needle for lighter weight, finer fabrics, and monofilament threads; use a larger number needle for medium-weight fabrics and cotton threads. Sewing on flannel or working with decorative threads requires larger or specialty needles.

 **3.** To end, stitch one or two threads past the point where the stitching began and take one or two backstitches to secure the thread. (If your machine has a variable stitch length, you may wish to set your stitch length at 0 and take a few stitches, one on top of the next, to lock the threads in place.)

# Satin or Zigzag Stitch Appliqué

Variable-width satin or zigzag stitch makes a smooth, professional-looking finish on appliqué edges. Choose a thread color that complements or matches your appliqué fabric. Select a stitch width that corresponds to the size of the piece being appliquéd. Larger pieces can accommodate a wider, denser appliqué stitch than smaller appliqué shapes can.

With a machine satin stitch, it is not necessary to turn under the appliqué piece's edges because the entire outer edge is held in place by the zigzag or satin stitch. The outer edge of the stitch just grazes the appliqué foundation. Depending upon the stability of your fabric, the appliqué design, and your personal preference, you can use fusible web, pins, or fabric glue to hold the appliqué pieces in place for machine stitching. Use a stabilizer behind the appliqué foundation.

## Sewing Machine Setup for Machine Appliqué

- Make certain your machine is clean and in good working order.

- Install a new size 60/8, 70/10, 75/11, or 80/12 sharp embroidery needle in your machine.

- Wind a bobbin with cotton 60-weight embroidery thread or bobbin-fill thread.

- Thread the needle with matching- or complementary-color cotton 60-weight embroidery thread.

- Set your machine for a zigzag stitch with a width between 1 and 1.5mm or about ⅛" wide. Set the stitch length just above (not at) the satin-stitch setting, or between .5 and 1mm.

- If possible, set your machine in the "needle down" position, and set the motor at half speed.

**1.** Position the presser foot so that the left swing of the needle is on the appliqué and the right swing of the needle is just on the outer edge of the appliqué, grazing the appliqué foundation.

**2.** Begin stitching on a curve or straight edge, not at an inner or outer point.

## PIVOTING AT CORNERS, CURVES, AND POINTS

The position of your needle is critical when pivoting fabric to round a curve or turn a point or corner. Use the following illustrations to guide you in knowing when to pivot. In each case, you will need to place your needle down in the fabric before pivoting. In each illustration the arrows indicate stitching direction, and the dots mark where the needle should be down for pivoting.

### Turning Corners–Method 1

With this method the stitches cross over one another in the corners.

**1.** Stop with the needle down in the fabric on the right-hand swing of the needle.

**2.** Raise the presser foot and pivot the fabric. Lower the presser foot and begin stitching to the next edge.

### Turning Corners–Method 2

With this method the stitching lines abut, but they do not cross over one another.

**1.** Stop with the needle down in the fabric on the left-hand swing of the needle.

**2.** Raise the presser foot and pivot the fabric. Lower the presser foot and turn the handwheel until the right-hand swing of the needle is just about to go into the foundation fabric. Lift the presser foot and reposition the foundation fabric so the tip of the needle is above the point where the needle thread is coming out of the appliqué. Lower the presser foot and begin stitching to the next edge.

# Appliqué Primer

### Pivoting Inside Curves

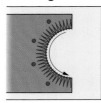

Stop at the first pivot point with the needle down in the fabric on the left-hand swing of the needle. Raise the presser foot, pivot the fabric slightly, and begin stitching to the next pivot point. Repeat as needed to round the entire inner curve.

### Pivoting Outside Curves

Stop at the first pivot point with the needle down in the fabric on the right-hand swing of the needle. Raise the presser foot, pivot the fabric slightly, and begin stitching to the next pivot point. Repeat as needed to round the entire outer curve.

### Pivoting Inside Points

**1.** With a marking tool, mark a line extending from the upcoming edge of the appliqué into the center. On the line, measure from the point a distance equal to your stitch width; mark the location with a dot.

**2.** Stitch to the bottom of the inside point, stopping with the needle down in the fabric on the left-hand swing of the needle. The needle should be at the dot on your drawn marked line.

**3.** Raise the presser foot and pivot the fabric. Lower the presser foot and turn the handwheel until the right-hand swing of the needle is just about to go into the foundation fabric. Lift the presser foot and reposition the foundation fabric so the tip of the needle is above the point where the needle thread is coming out of the appliqué. Lower the presser foot and begin stitching to the next edge.

### Pivoting Outside Points

Shapes with outside points are among the more difficult to appliqué. This method requires you to taper your stitch width at the point. If your project requires you to appliqué around this shape, practice first on scraps to perfect your technique.

**1.** Stitch along the first edge of the appliqué, keeping the stitch width consistent until the left-hand swing of the needle begins to touch the opposite outside edge of the point. Stop with the needle down in the fabric on the left-hand swing of the needle.

**2.** Gradually reduce your stitch width and continue sewing toward the point. Keep the right- and left-hand swings of the needle just grazing the outer edges and taper your stitch width until it's 0 at the point. Stop with the needle down in the fabric.

**3.** Raise the presser foot and pivot the fabric. Lower the presser foot and begin stitching away from the point, increasing the stitch width at the same rate that you decreased it until you have returned to the original stitch width. Pivot the fabric slightly as needed to keep the right-hand swing of the needle grazing the foundation at the right-hand edge of the appliqué piece.

# Mock Hand Appliqué

This method uses monofilament thread in the needle and the blind hem stitch to make virtually invisible stitches. *Note:* Contrasting thread was used in the photos that follow for illustration purposes only.

**1.** Prepare the appliqué pieces following Freezer-Paper Method 2.

**2.** Position an appliqué piece so that the needle goes into the appliqué foundation right next to it. The needle should be so near the fold of the appliqué piece that it touches the fold but does not stitch through it. When the needle jumps to the left, the stitch should be totally on the appliqué piece. When the needle jumps to the right to complete a zigzag stitch, the needle should again be against the edge of the appliqué piece but go through the foundation only.

**3.** When you come to inside and outside points, make sure to secure them with several stitches. Make certain the needle always touches the fold of the appliqué so no edges are missed.

**4.** Continue stitching around the appliqué. When you reach the location where the stitching began, stitch over the beginning stitches to secure the threads. To lock your stitches, backstitch only two or three stitches.

**5.** When the stitching is complete, check all the edges of the appliqué to make sure no areas were left unstitched. On the wrong side, carefully trim away the foundation fabric from within each stitched shape, leaving a ¼" seam allowance.

**6.** Using a spritzer bottle, spray water on the inside of the appliqué's seam allowances, making sure to wet the areas that were glued over the freezer paper.

**7.** Remove the paper. You'll find that once the water dissolves the glue, the freezer paper will slip right out.

**8.** When the freezer paper has been removed from all appliqués, place a thick bath towel atop your pressing surface and lay the appliqué facedown on the towel.

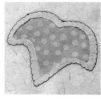

Cover the back of the appliqué with a pressing cloth; press with a warm iron. (The towel prevents the edges of the appliqués from being flattened by the iron.)

*Note:* Contrasting thread is used here for illustration purposes only.

If monofilament thread had been used, no stitching line would be visible on the right side of the fabric.

## Sewing Machine Setup for Mock Hand Appliqué

- Make certain your machine is clean and in good working order.

- Install a new size 60/8, 70/10, or 75/11 embroidery needle in your machine.

- Wind a bobbin with cotton 60-weight embroidery thread.

- Thread the needle with lightweight, invisible, nylon (monofilament) thread. Use clear thread for light-color fabrics; use smoke-color invisible thread for medium- and dark-color fabrics.

- Set your machine for a blind hem stitch with the stitch width and length each set at 1mm. This stitch takes 2 to 5 straight stitches, then a zigzag, then 2 to 5 more straight stitches before zigzagging again.

$$- \_ - \wedge \_ - \wedge \_ - \wedge \_ - \wedge \_ - \wedge \_ - \wedge \_ -$$

Stitch a test sample using the same threads and fabrics as in your project. The distance between each zigzag should be ⅛" maximum, and the width of the zigzag should be the width of two threads. When you are finished, you should be able to see the needle holes, but no thread. If you gently pull on the edge of the appliqué, the stitching should be strong and without gaps.

Check the stitch tension on the test sample. There should be no bobbin thread showing on the top and no loops of nylon thread on the bottom. If the bobbin thread is showing on the top, loosen the top tension gradually until the bobbin thread no longer shows. Turn the sample over. If there are loops of nylon thread on the bottom, you've loosened the top tension too much.

# Decorative Stitch Appliqué

This technique is often done on a sewing machine using the blanket stitch. Other decorative stitches also may be used, such as the featherstitch.

**1.** Prepare the appliqué pieces following the desired method. Pin, baste, or glue the appliqués in place.

**2.** Use a tear-away stabilizer beneath the appliqué foundation.

**3.** Beginning on a straight edge or a curve, take a few stitches; hold the thread tails out of the way to prevent thread snarls on the wrong side of your project. The right swing of the needle should graze the appliqué foundation. The left swing of the needle should be completely on the appliqué piece.

**4.** For inside curves, stop with the needle down in the fabric on the left needle swing, lift the presser foot, pivot the appliqué foundation, lower the presser foot, and continue sewing.

**5.** For outside curves, stop with the needle down in the fabric on the right needle swing, lift the presser foot, pivot the appliqué foundation, and continue sewing.

**6.** Adjust the stitch length as necessary at corners and where the stitching meets at the end.

---

**Sewing Machine Setup for Decorative Stitch Appliqué**

- Make certain your machine is clean and in good working order.

- Install a new size 80/14 embroidery needle in your machine.

- Wind a bobbin with cotton 60-weight embroidery thread in a neutral color.

- Thread the needle with matching- or contrasting-color cotton 60-weight embroidery thread. Use black cotton 40-weight embroidery thread in the needle for a folk art look.

- Set your machine for the desired stitch length and width.
  Stitch a test sample using the same thread and fabrics as your project. If your tension is properly adjusted, no bobbin thread will show on the top of your appliqué.

---

# Fusible-Web Appliqué

To finish the edges of appliqué pieces that have been fused to the appliqué foundation, follow the instructions for Satin or Zigzag Stitch Appliqué, Decorative Stitch Appliqué, or Embroidery Stitches. Be sure you have prepared your appliqués with a sew-through fusible web.

# Wool Appliqué

Felted wool—wool that has been napped and shrunk—is easy to work with because the edges will not ravel so there is no need to turn them under. Use templates to cut felted wool into appliqué pieces. Do not include seam allowances.

Use a basic running stitch or decorative hand- or machine-embroidery stitches to attach wool appliqués to an appliqué foundation. Or, for added dimension, tack wool appliqué pieces at their centers only.

To felt wool for use in appliqué, machine-wash it in a hot-water/cool-rinse cycle with a small amount of detergent, machine-dry, and steam-press. It is the disparity in temperatures, along with the agitation, that causes the wool to felt. If you wish to use wool from a piece of clothing, cut it apart and remove the seams so it can shrink freely.

# Embroidery Stitches

## BLANKET STITCH

To blanket-stitch, refer to the diagram *below*. First pull the needle up at A, form a reverse L shape with the floss, and hold the angle of the L shape in place with your thumb. Then push the needle down at B and come up at C to secure the stitch. Continue in the same manner, pushing the needle down at D and up at E, until you've gone completely around the piece.

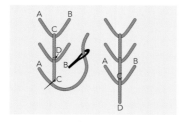

Blanket Stitch

## FLY STITCH

To fly-stitch (see diagram *below*), pull the needle up at A, form a V shape with the thread, and hold the angle in place with your thumb. Push the needle down at B, about ³⁄₁₆" from A, and come up at C. (The V shape can point in either direction.) For the next stitch, insert the needle at D and bring it out at A.

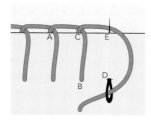

Fly Stitch

## STEM STITCH

To stem-stitch, refer to the diagram *below*. First pull the needle up at A. Insert the needle into the fabric at B, about ³⁄₈" away from A. Holding the thread out of the way, bring the needle back up at C and pull the thread through so it lies flat against the fabric. The distances between points A, B, and C should be equal. Pull with equal tautness after each stitch.

Stem Stitch

## RUNNING STITCH

To make a running stitch, pull your needle up at A (see diagram *below*) and insert it back into the fabric at B, ⅛" away from A. Pull your needle up at C, ⅛" from B, and repeat.

Running Stitch

## CROSS-STITCH

To cross-stitch, pull the needle up at A (see diagram *below*), then push it down at B. Bring the needle up at C, cross over the first stitch, and push the needle down at D to make an X.

Cross-stitch

## HERRINGBONE STITCH

To herringbone-stitch, pull your needle up at A (see diagram *below*), then insert it back into the fabric at B. Bring your needle up at C, cross the floss over the first stitch, and push your needle down at D. Pull your needle up at E, cross the floss over the second stitch, and push your needle down at F. Pull your needle up at G and continue in the same manner.

Herringbone Stitch

## SATIN STITCH

To satin-stitch, see diagram *below*. Use a quilter's pencil to outline the area you want to cover. Then fill in the area with straight stitches, stitching from edge to edge and placing the stitches side by side.

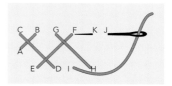

Satin Stitch

## BACKSTITCH

To backstitch, pull your needle up at A (see diagram *below*). Insert it back into the fabric at B, and bring it up at C. Push your needle down again at D, and bring it up at E. Continue in the same manner.

Backstitch

# Traditional
# Needle-Turn
# Appliqué

It's the original technique: Hand stitching around a precut shape to embellish a larger piece of contrasting fabric. From primitive to contemporary, this art fits every style.

It's easier—and faster—with felted wool: The edges don't fray, so there is no need to turn under a hem. And the fabric is a joy to work with.

So get started now, and create a tradition of your own: Simple quilts with hand-sewn appliqué embellishments to commemorate special events and holidays.

Peaceful doves fly from a base of mosaic fabric:
scraps of similar colors, sewn together and then
cut as a single piece.

# Wreath of Doves

## MATERIALS
1 yard total of assorted blue prints for
    appliqué foundation
1 yard total of assorted white prints
    for dove appliqués and border
½ yard total of assorted red prints for
    berry appliqués and border
½ yard total of assorted green prints
    for leaf appliqués
⅓ yard of gold print for binding
1 yard of backing fabric
36" square of quilt batting

Finished quilt top: 30" square

Quantities specified for 44/45"-wide,
100% cotton fabrics. All
measurements include a ¼" seam
allowance. Sew with right sides
together unless otherwise stated.

Design: Sharon Reid Williams
Photographs: Perry Struse;
    Marcia Cameron

## SELECT THE FABRICS
The assorted blue, white, red, and
green prints are used for mosaic
quilting. When choosing fabrics in
a particular color group for mosaic
quilting, designer Shannon Reid
Williams says to be sure and include
a variety of shades and patterns.

# Wreath of Doves

## USE THE MOSAIC-QUILTING METHOD

**1.** Cut the assorted blue, white, red, and green prints into smaller pieces. The blue prints should be cut into pieces of varying sizes, both small and large, because they will be pieced into the appliqué foundation. The white, red, and green prints should be cut into only small pieces because they will be pieced into a rectangle, then cut into the appliqué shapes.

**2.** Sew together the blue print pieces in a random fashion, cutting and re-sewing as needed, to create four blue mosaic 13½" squares, including the seam allowances.

**3.** In the same manner, sew the white print pieces into a white mosaic 24×42" rectangle.

**4.** Sew the red print pieces into a red mosaic 12×28" rectangle.

**5.** Sew the green print pieces into a green mosaic 12×22" rectangle.

## CUT THE FABRICS

To make the best use of your fabrics, cut the pieces in the order that follows. The patterns are on *page 20*. To make templates of the patterns, follow the instructions in Appliqué Primer, which begins on *page 2*. Remember to add a ³⁄₁₆" seam allowance when cutting out the appliqué pieces.

*From white mosaic 24×42" rectangle, cut:*
- 28—2½" squares
- 8 of Pattern A

*From red mosaic 12×28" rectangle, cut:*
- 28—2½" squares
- 16 of Pattern B

*From green mosaic 12×22" rectangle, cut:*
- 40 of Pattern C

*From gold print, cut:*
- 4—2¼×42" binding strips

## ASSEMBLE THE QUILT TOP

**1.** Sew together the four blue mosaic 13½" squares in two rows. Press the seam allowances in opposite directions. Then join the rows to make the quilt center. The pieced quilt center should measure 26½" square, including the seam allowances.

**2.** Sew together seven white mosaic 2½" squares and six red mosaic 2½" squares, alternating colors, to make a short border unit. Press the seam allowances toward the red squares.

The pieced short border unit should measure 2½×26½", including the seam allowances. Repeat to make a second short border unit. Sew the short border units to opposite edges of the quilt center. Press the seam allowances toward the border.

**3.** Sew together seven white mosaic 2½" squares and eight red mosaic 2½" squares, alternating colors, to make a long border unit. Press the seam allowances toward the red squares. The pieced long border unit should measure 2½×30½", including the seam allowances. Repeat to make a second long border unit. Sew the long border units to the remaining edges of the quilt center to complete the quilt top. Press the seam allowances toward the border.

## APPLIQUÉ THE QUILT TOP

**1.** Referring to the photograph *opposite* for placement, position all the appliqué shapes on the quilt top. When you are pleased with the arrangement, baste in place.

**2.** Using threads in colors that match the fabrics, appliqué the pieces to the quilt top.

**3.** After the appliquéing is complete, cut away the excess fabric behind each appliquéd piece.

## COMPLETE THE QUILT

**1.** Layer the quilt top, batting, and backing according to the instructions in Quilting Basics, which begins on *page 94*.

**2.** Quilt as desired. Shannon hand-quilted a 2¾"-wide diagonal grid in the quilt center. Then she outline-quilted each dove appliqué.

**3.** Use the gold print 2¼×42" strips to bind the quilt according to the instructions in Quilting Basics.

## SPRING FLIGHT

In anticipation of spring, choose pastel fabrics for a different version of this project. First use the mosaic-quilting method to make a 10½×14½" appliqué foundation. Then appliqué a white dove and assorted red berries and green leaves atop the rectangle. Finish the small wall hanging by adding a scrappy border.

# Wreath of Doves

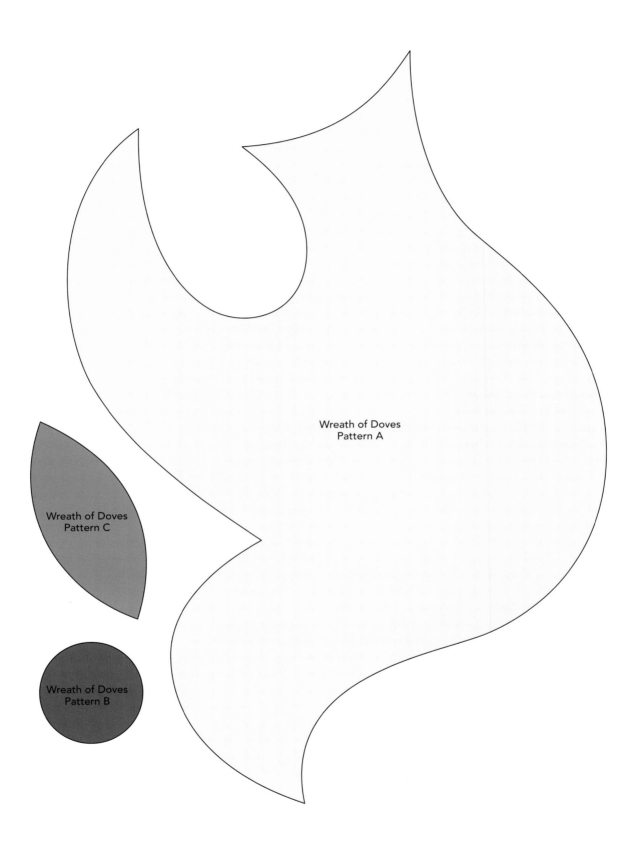

Wreath of Doves
Pattern A

Wreath of Doves
Pattern C

Wreath of Doves
Pattern B

Almost abstract, this is an angel for all times.
Make it from your favorite scraps, or in colors the
lucky recipient likes best!

# Heavenly Angel

## MATERIALS

13" square of tan print for appliqué foundation

¼ yard of tan stripe for blocks

6—⅛-yard pieces of assorted dark brown stripes and plaids for blocks

9×22" (fat eighth) of solid green for stem and leaf appliqués

⅜ yard of gold print for angel dress appliqué and binding

6" square of rust print for flower appliqué

4" square of gold plaid for flower center appliqué

5" square of tan plaid for angel wing appliqué

Scrap of solid beige for angel face appliqué

Scrap of solid brown for angel hair appliqué

⅔ yard of backing fabric

24×26" of quilt batting

Freezer paper

Finished quilt top: 20×17½"

Quantities specified for 44/45"-wide, 100% cotton fabrics. All measurements include a ¼" seam allowance. Sew with right sides together unless otherwise stated.

Design: Terri Degenkolb and
   Jackie Conaway
Photographs: Perry Struse;
   Craig Anderson

## CUT THE FABRICS

To make the best use of your fabrics, cut the pieces in the order that follows. The patterns are on *page 24.*

To use freezer paper for appliquéing, as was done in this project, complete the following steps.

**1.** Lay the freezer paper, shiny side down, over the patterns. Use a pencil to trace the pattern the number of times indicated, leaving a ¼" space between tracings. Cut out each piece on the traced lines.

**2.** Press the freezer-paper shapes onto the wrong sides of the fabrics as designated, leaving ½" between shapes. Let the fabrics cool. Cut out fabric shapes roughly ¼" beyond the freezer-paper edges.

**3.** Finger-press the seam allowances around the edges of the freezer-paper shapes.

*From tan stripe, cut:*
- 3—3⅜" squares, cutting each diagonally in half for a total of 6 large triangles (You'll have 1 leftover.)
- 18—1¾×3" rectangles
- 12—2⅛" squares, cutting each diagonally in half for a total of 24 small triangles
- 8—1¾" squares

*From assorted dark brown stripes and plaids, cut:*
- 5—3⅜" squares, cutting each diagonally in half to make a total of 10 large triangles (You'll use 1 triangle from each fabric.)
- 8—1¾×3" rectangles

*From each of four assorted dark brown stripes or plaids, cut:*
- 1—1¾×3" rectangle
- 2—2⅛" squares, cutting each diagonally in half for a total of 4 small triangles

*From each of two assorted dark brown stripes or plaids, cut:*
- 2—1¾×3" rectangles
- 2—2⅛" squares, cutting each diagonally in half for a total of 4 small triangles
- 2—1¾" squares

# Heavenly Angel

*From solid green, cut:*
- 1—1½×20" bias strip (For specific instructions on cutting bias strips, see Appliqué Primer, which begins on *page 2.*)
- 1 of Pattern C

*From gold print, cut:*
- 2—2½×42" binding strips
- 1 of Pattern D

*From rust print, cut:*
- 1 of Pattern A

*From gold plaid, cut:*
- 1 of Pattern B

*From tan plaid, cut:*
- 1 of Pattern E

*From solid beige, cut:*
- 1 of Pattern F

*From solid brown, cut:*
- 1 of Pattern G

## APPLIQUÉ THE CENTER SQUARE

**1.** Fold the solid green 1½×20" bias strip in half lengthwise with the wrong side inside. Using a ¼" seam allowance, sew down the length of the strip (see Diagram 1). Roll the strip so the seam is in the middle of one side; press flat to make a stem appliqué.

Diagram 1

**2.** Referring to the Quilt Assembly Diagram, arrange the prepared appliqué shapes atop the tan print 13" appliqué foundation square.

To position appliqué pieces squarely on the foundation, fold the foundation in half vertically and horizontally to determine the center. Lightly finger-press along the folds to create four positioning lines. Then pencil in four equal sections on the Quilt Assembly Diagram so you can better judge exactly where appliqué pieces should be placed on the foundation.

**3.** Working from the bottom layer up and using threads in colors that match the appliqués, hand- or machine-appliqué each shape in place, leaving a ½" opening in each. Using the opening for access, remove the templates by sliding your needle between the fabric and freezer paper. Gently loosen and pull out the freezer-paper templates. Stitch the openings closed to complete the appliquéd center square.

## ASSEMBLE THE TRIANGLE-SQUARES

**1.** Referring to Diagram 2 for placement, sew together a large tan stripe triangle and a large dark brown stripe or plaid triangle to make a large triangle-square. Press the seam allowance toward the dark brown triangle. The pieced large triangle-square should measure 3" square, including the seam allowance. Repeat to make a total of five large triangle-squares.

Diagram 2

**2.** In the same manner, sew together a small tan stripe triangle and a small brown stripe or plaid triangle

Quilt Assembly Diagram

to make a small triangle-square. Press the seam allowance toward the dark brown triangle (see Diagram 3). The pieced small triangle-square should measure 1¾" square, including the seam allowance. Repeat to make a total of 24 small triangle-squares.

Diagram 3

### ASSEMBLE THE CHURN DASH BLOCKS

**1.** Referring to Diagram 4 on *page 25* for placement, lay out one

tan stripe 1¾×3" rectangle, two dark brown stripe 1¾" squares, two dark brown stripe or plaid 1¾×3" rectangles, and four small triangle-squares with the same dark brown stripe or plaid in three horizontal rows.

# Heavenly Angel

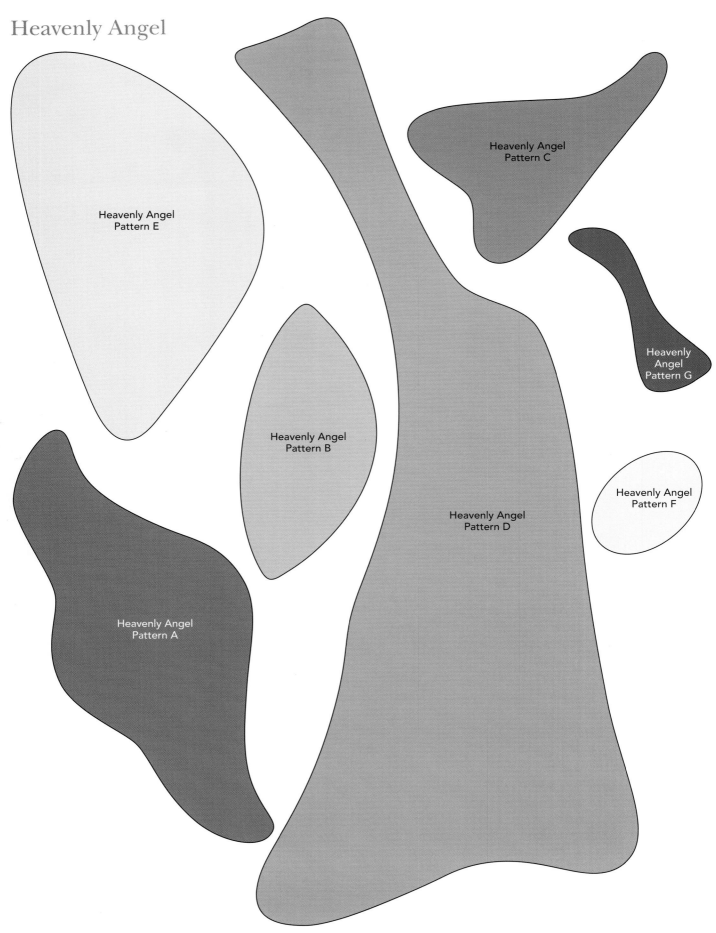

Heavenly Angel
Pattern E

Heavenly Angel
Pattern C

Heavenly Angel
Pattern B

Heavenly
Angel
Pattern G

Heavenly Angel
Pattern F

Heavenly Angel
Pattern D

Heavenly Angel
Pattern A

Diagram 4

**2.** Sew together the pieces in each row. Press the seam allowances toward the dark brown stripe squares and rectangles. Then join the rows to make a dark Churn Dash block. Press the seam allowances in one direction. The pieced dark Churn Dash block should measure 4¼×5½", including the seam allowances.

**3.** Repeat steps 1 and 2 to make a second dark Churn Dash block.

**4.** Referring to Diagram 5 for placement, lay out two tan stripe 1¾×3" rectangles, two tan stripe 1¾" squares, a dark brown stripe or plaid 1¾×3" rectangle, and four small triangle-squares with the same dark brown stripe or plaid in three horizontal rows.

Diagram 5

**5.** Sew together the pieces in each row. Press the seam allowances toward the tan stripe pieces. Then join the rows to make a light Churn Dash block. Press the seam allowances in one direction. The pieced light Churn Dash block should measure 4¼×5½", including the seam allowances.

**6.** Repeat steps 4 and 5 to make a total of four light Churn Dash blocks.

## ASSEMBLE THE QUILT TOP

**1.** Referring to the Quilt Assembly Diagram on *page 22* for placement, lay out the appliquéd center square, the five large triangle-squares, the six Churn Dash blocks, the eight tan stripe 1¾×3" rectangles, and the eight dark brown stripe or plaid 1¾×3" rectangles in sections.

**2.** Sew together the large triangle-squares in a row, pressing the seam allowances in one direction. Join the triangle-square row to the top edge of the appliquéd center square. Press the seam allowances toward the center square.

**3.** Sew together the Churn Dash blocks on each side to make two rows; press the seam allowances in one direction. Join a row to each side edge of the appliquéd center square. Press the seam allowances toward the center square.

**4.** Join the eight tan stripe rectangles and eight dark brown stripe or plaid rectangles in two horizontal rows, alternating light and dark rectangles. Press the seam allowances toward the dark rectangles. Join the rows to make a rectangle unit; press the seam allowances in one direction. Add the rectangle unit to the bottom edge of the appliquéd center square; press the seam allowances toward the rectangle unit to complete the quilt top.

## COMPLETE THE QUILT

**1.** Layer the quilt top, batting, and backing according to the instructions in Quilting Basics, which begins on *page 94*. Quilt as desired.

**2.** Use the gold print 2½×42" strips to bind the quilt according to the instructions in Quilting Basics.

## CHRISTMAS ANGELS

Use the angel motif to decorate a felt 49"-diameter Christmas tree skirt with fused felt appliqués. Replace the flower motif with a simple star shape at the top and rectangles of green felt for tree branches. Add buttons to the tree for extra detail.

# Folk Art Horse

Atop a combination of wool, flannel, and cotton fabrics, with double appliqué seams, this horse is fine folk art.

## MATERIALS

⅜ yard of black wool for appliqué foundation
Scraps of black-and-white plaid for corners
⅓ yard of taupe flannel for appliqué
18×22" piece (fat quarter) of gold print for inner border
18×22" piece (fat quarter) of black-and-white check for outer border
18×22" piece (fat quarter) each of olive, rust, and taupe prints for braided trim
17" square of backing fabric
2 yards of black-and-taupe cording
Olive green embroidery floss
16" pillow form

Finished pillow cover: 16½" square

Quantities specified for 44/45"-wide, 100% cotton fabrics. All measurements include a ¼" seam allowance. Sew with right sides together unless otherwise stated.

Design: Miriam Gourley
Photographs: Perry Struse;
    Craig Anderson

## CUT THE FABRICS

To make the best use of your fabrics, cut the pieces in the order that follows. The pattern is on *page 28*. Make the pattern full-size. To make a template of the pattern, follow the instructions in Appliqué Primer, which begins on *page 2*.

*From black wool, cut:*
- 1—12½" square for appliqué foundation

*From black-and-white plaid, cut:*
- 4—2⅞" squares

*From taupe flannel, cut:*
- 1—10×30" rectangle

*From gold print, cut:*
- 2—1¼×14" inner border strips
- 2—1¼×12½" inner border strips

*From black-and-white check, cut:*
- 2—2×17" outer border strips
- 2—2×14" outer border strips

*From each of the olive, rust, and taupe prints, cut:*
- 5—1×22" strips

## ASSEMBLE THE APPLIQUÉ FOUNDATION

**1.** For accurate sewing lines, use a quilter's pencil to mark a diagonal line on the wrong side of the black-and-white plaid 2⅞" squares. (To prevent your fabric from stretching as you draw the lines, place 220-grit sandpaper under the squares.)

**2.** Pin a black-and-white plaid 2⅞" square to each corner of the black wool appliqué foundation (see Diagram 1; note the placement of the marked diagonal lines). Stitch on the marked lines; trim the seam allowances to ¼". Press the attached triangles open to make the appliqué foundation (see Diagram 2).

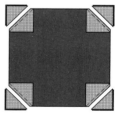

Diagram 1

Diagram 2

## ASSEMBLE THE PILLOW CENTER

**1.** Fold the taupe flannel 10×30" rectangle in half, right sides together, bringing the short sides together, and pin or baste around the edges. Use a marking pencil to trace around the horse template on the folded fabric. The marking will be the stitching line.

To reduce bulk when making double-appliqué pieces, use sheer, featherweight, nonfusible, nonwoven interfacing for the underside of the appliqué piece.

After stitching the interfacing and fabric together, trim the interfacing seam allowance slightly smaller than the appliqué fabric before turning it right side out. The seam allowance will roll slightly to the back of the appliqué and won't be visible when you stitch the appliqué to its foundation.

**2.** Carefully machine-stitch on the marked line. Trim around the stitching, leaving a ¼" seam allowance. Clip any angles or curves, taking care not to clip the stitching.

**3.** Carefully make a slit in the top layer of the fabric. Turn the horse appliqué piece right side out, and push out any corners or angles. Press the piece and baste it to the center of the pieced appliqué foundation.

**4.** Using matching thread and slip stitches, appliqué the horse to the pieced appliqué foundation to complete the pillow center.

# Folk Art Horse

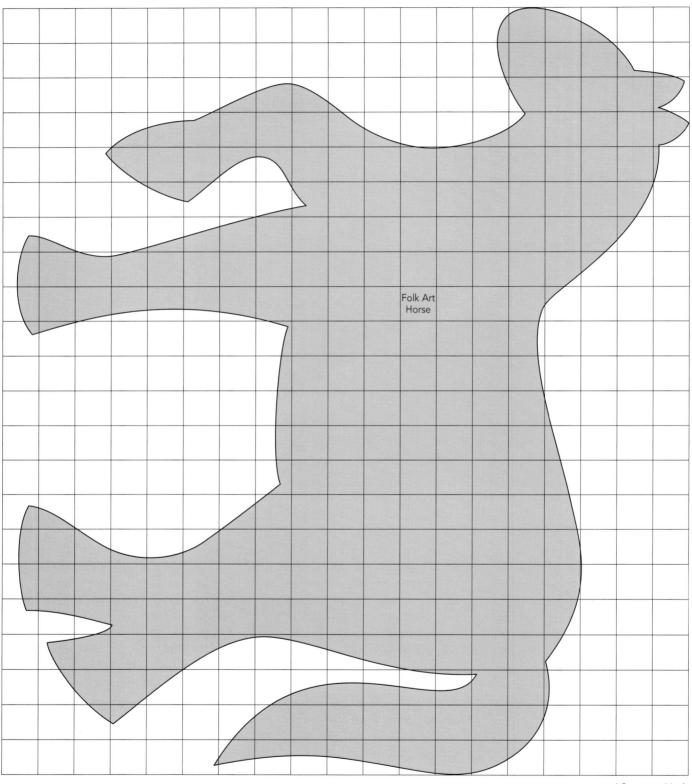

Folk Art
Horse

1 Square = 1 Inch

## ADD THE BORDERS

**1.** Sew the gold print 1¼×12½" inner border strips to opposite edges of the pillow center. Press the seam allowances toward the border.

**2.** Sew the gold print 1¼×14" inner border strips to the remaining edges of the pillow center. Press the seam allowances toward the border.

**3.** Sew the black-and-white check 2×14" outer border strips to opposite edges of the pillow center. Press the seam allowances toward the check border.

**4.** Sew the black-and-white check 2×17" outer border strip to the remaining edges of the pillow center to complete the pillow top. Press the seam allowances toward the check border. The pieced pillow top should measure 17" square, including the seam allowances.

## COMPLETE THE PILLOW

**1.** Referring to the photograph on *page 27*, use six strands of olive green embroidery floss to fly-stitch the pillow top. For instructions on making the fly stitch, see the Appliqué Primer, which begins on *page 2.*

**2.** Sew the five olive print 1×22" strips together, short end to short end, to make a pieced strip that is 108" long. Repeat with the rust print 1×22" strips and taupe print 1×22" strips.

**3.** Braid the strips together until the braid is about 72" long. Place the braid around the outside edge of the gold print border. Slip-stitch the braid to the pillow top, overlapping the ends and tucking the raw edges underneath.

**4.** Pin the black-and-taupe cording to the pillow top with the flat side of the cording along the raw edges. Clip the cording at the corners (see Diagram 3). Use a zipper foot to stitch the cording to the pillow top.

Diagram 3

**5.** Sew together the pillow top and pillow backing, sewing on the Step 4 stitching line. Leave an opening for the pillow form along a side edge. Clip the corners and turn the cover right side out.

**6.** Insert the pillow form through the opening. Whipstitch the opening closed.

## GOING IN CIRCLES

Incorporate the idea of braiding strips of fat quarters to create focal points for other pillow tops. For this batik pillow, we chose three fat quarters: a tone-on-tone black print, a tone-on-tone white print, and a black-and-white print. For each color, we stitched together four 1×22" strips to make a strip about 86" long. To attach the 54"-long braid, we pinned the spiral on the pillow top and tacked it in place by stitching from the wrong side. At each end of the braid, we tucked in the raw edges for a smooth finish.

The simple beauty of tulips abloom is reflected in the gentle curves and soft contours of the quilting on this coverlet.

# Tulips for Kelly

## MATERIALS

7 yards of solid ecru for foundation blocks, corner triangles, setting triangles, center setting square, border, and backing
1 yard of green stripe for border
2—¼-yard pieces of yellow floral for tulip appliqués
⅛ yard of pink polka dot for bow appliqués
¾ yard of solid green for stems, border corners, and binding
⅛ yard of green print for leaves
68" square of quilt batting

Finished quilt top: 62" square
Finished block: 13" square

Quantities specified for 44/45"-wide, 100% cotton fabrics. All measurements include a ¼" seam allowance. Sew with right sides together unless otherwise stated.

Design: Suzanne Mayberry
Photograph: Hopkins Associates

## CUT THE FABRICS

To make the best use of your fabrics, cut the pieces in the order that follows. For this project, cut the border strips lengthwise (parallel to the selvage). The patterns are on *page 33*. To make templates of the patterns, follow the instructions in Appliqué Primer, which begins on *page 2*.

*From solid ecru, cut:*
- 2—34¼×68" rectangles for backing
- 2—10×62½" border strips
- 2—10×43½" border strips
- 4—14½" squares for foundation blocks
- 2—13⅞" squares, cutting each diagonally in half for a total of 4 setting triangles
- 1—13½" center setting square
- 2—10⅛" squares, cutting each diagonally in half for a total of 4 corner triangles

*From green stripe, cut:*
- 4—3½×37½" bias strips (For specific instructions on cutting bias strips, see Appliqué Primer.)

*From each of the yellow florals, cut:*
- 6 of pattern A

*From pink polka dot, cut:*
- 4 *each* of patterns B, C, D, E, and F

*From solid green, cut:*
- 1—20×42" rectangle, cutting enough 2¼"-wide bias strips to total 268" in length for the binding; 8—1×8½" stem strips; and 4—1×9¾" stem strips
- 4—3½" border corner squares

*From green print, cut:*
- 4 *each* of patterns G and G reversed

## APPLIQUÉ THE BLOCKS

**1.** Fold a foundation square in half diagonally in both directions and lightly finger-crease to create positioning guides for the appliqué pieces.

**2.** Prepare appliqué pieces by basting a ³⁄₁₆" seam allowance. Do not baste under seam allowances that will be covered by another piece.

**3.** For stems, press under ¼" along each long edge of the solid green bias strips.

**4.** Pin or hand-baste two 8½" strips and one 9¾" strip onto a foundation square for stems (see the Block Assembly Diagram for placement). Then pin the tulips, leaves, and bow pieces in place. To reduce bulk, trim the stems so that just ¼" runs under the tulip and bow appliqués.

Block Assembly Diagram

**5.** Using small slip stitches and threads in colors that match the fabrics, appliqué the pieces in place starting with the stems, then the tulips and leaves, and finishing with the bow. Always work from the bottom layer to the top layer. Repeat to make a total of four blocks. Trim the blocks as needed to 13½" square, including the seam allowances.

## ASSEMBLE THE QUILT CENTER

**1.** Lay out the four appliquéd blocks, the center setting square, the setting triangles, and the corner triangles in diagonal rows as shown in the Quilt Assembly Diagram.

**2.** Join the blocks, except the corner triangles, into rows. Press the seam allowances toward the setting triangles and center setting square. Join the rows. Press the seam allowances in one direction. Add the corner triangles to make the quilt center. Press the seam allowances toward the corner triangles. The pieced quilt center should measure 37½" square, including the seam allowances.

## ADD THE BORDERS

**1.** Sew the green stripe 3½×37½" bias strips to opposite edges of the quilt center. To each end of the remaining green stripe bias strips add a solid green 3½" square.

Then add the bias strips to the remaining edges of the quilt center. Press all seam allowances toward the bias strips.

**2.** Sew the solid ecru 10×43½" border strips to opposite edges of the quilt center. Then add the solid ecru 10×62½" border strips to the remaining edges of the quilt center to complete the quilt top. Press all seam allowances toward the solid ecru border strips.

## COMPLETE THE QUILT

**1.** Layer the quilt top, batting, and backing according to the instructions in Quilting Basics, which begins on *page 94.*

Quilt Assembly Diagram

**2.** Quilt as desired. Suzanne outline hand-quilted all of the appliqué pieces. Then she hand-quilted 12"-diameter feathered circles and 1"-wide straight lines in the center setting squares, setting triangles, and corner triangles. She hand-quilted a cable design in the green stripe border, and a scalloped feather design and 1"-wide straight lines in the solid ecru border.

**3.** Use the solid green 2¼" bias strips to bind the quilt according to the instructions in Quilting Basics.

*Note:* If you choose to scallop the edge of the quilt, do not quilt completely to the outside edge of the solid ecru border. Instead bind the quilt, following the feathered scallop design.

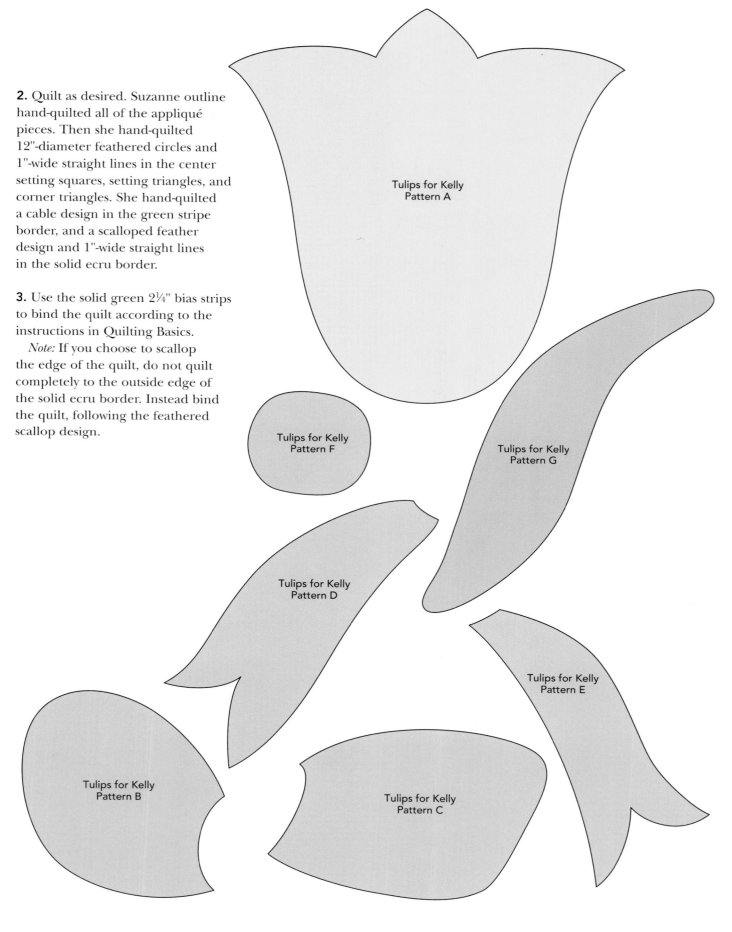

Tulips for Kelly
Pattern A

Tulips for Kelly
Pattern F

Tulips for Kelly
Pattern G

Tulips for Kelly
Pattern D

Tulips for Kelly
Pattern E

Tulips for Kelly
Pattern B

Tulips for Kelly
Pattern C

Amid a border of bowties, poppies seem to spring from the large beige triangles of a radiant Flying Geese block.

# Passion for Poppies

## MATERIALS

⅓ yard of solid beige for center block

¾ yard of navy plaid for center block, inner border, and binding

⅛ yard of gold stripe for center block and inner border

½ yard of green plaid for leaves, stems, calyx, and inner border

⅛ yard of gold plaid for center block and inner border

¼ yard of solid red for poppies and outer border

⅛ yard of red plaid for center block and outer border

3—⅛-yard pieces of red plaid for outer border

1 yard of backing fabric

36" square of quilt batting

1 skein of perle cotton No. 8: taupe

1 yard of freezer paper

Finished quilt top: 29½" square

Quantities specified for 44/45"-wide, 100% cotton fabrics. All measurements include a ¼" seam allowance. Sew with right sides together unless otherwise stated.

Design: Kris Kerrigan
Photographs: Perry Struse;
    Hopkins Associates

## CUT THE FABRICS

To make the best use of your fabrics, cut the pieces in the order that follows. The patterns are on *page 38*.

To use freezer paper for appliquéing, as was done in this project, complete the following steps.

**1.** Lay the freezer paper, shiny side down, over the patterns. Use a pencil to trace the pattern the number of times indicated, leaving a ¼" space between tracings. Cut out each piece on the traced lines.

**2.** Press the freezer-paper shapes onto the wrong sides of the fabrics as designated below, leaving ½" between shapes. Let the fabrics cool. Cut out fabric shapes roughly ¼" beyond the freezer-paper edges.

**3.** Finger-press the seam allowances around the edges of the freezer-paper shapes.

*From solid beige, cut:*
- 2—9⅜" squares, cutting each in half diagonally for a total of 4 triangles
- 4—4½" squares

*From navy plaid, cut:*
- 4—2½×42" binding strips
- 4—6⅞" squares, cutting each in half diagonally for a total of 8 large triangles
- 4—3" squares, cutting each in half diagonally for a total of 8 small triangles
- 8—2⅝" squares
- 16—2½" squares

*From gold stripe, cut:*
- 8—2½×4½" rectangles
- 4—2⅞" squares, cutting each in half diagonally for a total of 8 triangles

*From green plaid, cut:*
- 2—1×14" strips
- 4—5⅛" squares, cutting each in half diagonally for a total of 8 large triangles
- 4—3⅝" squares, cutting each in half diagonally for a total of 8 medium triangles
- 2—2⅞" squares, cutting each in half diagonally for a total of 4 small triangles
- 4—2½" squares
- 4 *each* of patterns B, B reversed, and C

*From gold plaid, cut:*
- 1—4½" square
- 4—3" squares, cutting each in half diagonally for a total of 8 triangles

*From solid red, cut:*
- 1—3½×27" strip
- 4 of Pattern A

*From red plaid, cut:*
- 1—3½×27" strip
- 4—2½" squares

*From each of the remaining three red plaids, cut:*
- 1—3½×27" strip

**ASSEMBLE THE CENTER BLOCK**

**1.** For accurate sewing lines, use a pencil to mark a diagonal line on the wrong side of the navy plaid and red plaid 2½" squares.

**2.** Referring to Diagram 1 for placement, place two red plaid 2½" squares on opposite corners of the gold plaid 4½" square. Sew on the marked diagonal lines. Trim the seam allowances to ¼" and press the attached triangles open.

Diagram 1

**3.** Place red plaid 2½" squares on the remaining corners of the gold plaid 4½" square (see Diagram 2). Stitch on the marked diagonal lines. Trim the seam allowances to ¼" and press open to make a center square.

Diagram 2

**4.** Referring to Diagram 3 for placement, place a navy plaid 2½" square on one end of a gold stripe 2½×4½" rectangle. Stitch on the marked diagonal line; trim and press as before. Place a second navy plaid 2½" square on the other end of the gold stripe 2½×4½" rectangle; stitch, trim, and press to make a Flying Geese unit. Repeat to make a total of eight Flying Geese units.

Diagram 3

**5.** Referring to Diagram 4 for placement, lay out the eight Flying Geese units, the center square, and four solid beige 4½" squares in three vertical rows. Sew together the pieces in each row. Press the seam allowances toward the solid beige squares or the center square. Then join the rows to make a center unit. Press the seam allowances in one direction. The pieced center unit should measure 12½" square, including the seam allowances.

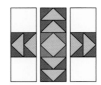

Diagram 4

**6.** Referring to Diagram 5 for placement, sew two solid beige triangles to opposite edges of the center unit. Press the seam allowances toward the solid beige

triangles. Sew the remaining solid beige triangles to the remaining edges of the center unit to make the center block. The pieced center block should measure 17½" square, including the seam allowances.

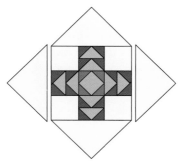

Diagram 5

## APPLIQUÉ THE CENTER BLOCK

**1.** Referring to Diagram 9 on *page 38* for placement, lay out the appliqué pieces on the pieced center block. When you're pleased with the arrangement, baste the pieces in place.

**2.** Using threads in colors that match the fabrics, appliqué the leaves in place first, leaving a ½" opening in each. Remove the freezer paper by sliding the needle into each opening between the freezer paper and the fabric. Gently loosen and pull out the freezer-paper templates. Slip-stitch the openings closed.

**3.** Press the two green plaid 1×14" strips in half lengthwise, then in half again to make stems. Appliqué the stems on the center block, crossing them in the center and covering the appliquéd leaf ends.

**4.** Using thread in a color that matches the fabric, appliqué the poppies in place, leaving the bottom

edges open. Remove the freezer paper as before; stitch openings closed.

**5.** Appliqué the calyxes in place next, covering the ends of the stems and poppies and leaving a ½" opening in each. Remove the freezer paper as before. Stitch the openings closed.

## ASSEMBLE AND ADD THE INNER BORDER

**1.** Sew together one gold stripe triangle, one green plaid small triangle, and one green plaid medium triangle; press (see Diagram 6). Then join one green plaid 2½" square, one green plaid medium triangle, and one gold stripe triangle as shown; press. Sew together to make a butterfly unit. Press the seam allowances in one direction.

Diagram 6

**2.** Referring to Diagram 7 for placement, sew a navy plaid large triangle to both sides of the butterfly units. Sew the green plaid large triangles to the navy plaid large triangles to make an inner border strip. Press the seam allowances in one direction.

Diagram 7

**3.** Repeat steps 1 and 2 to make a total of four inner border strips. Sew the inner border strips to the opposite edges of the center block (see Diagram 9 on *page 38*).

**4.** Referring to Diagram 8 for placement, sew together a navy plaid small triangle and a gold plaid triangle to make a triangle-square. Press the seam allowance in one direction. Add a navy plaid 2⅝" square to a triangle-square to make a subunit; press. Repeat to make a second subunit. Join the subunits to make a corner butterfly block. Press the seam allowance in one direction.

Diagram 8

**5.** Repeat Step 4 to make a total of four corner butterfly blocks.

**6.** Sew the corner butterfly blocks to the ends of the remaining inner border strips (see Diagram 9); press.

Sew the inner border strips to the remaining edges of the center block. Press the seam allowances in one direction.

Diagram 9

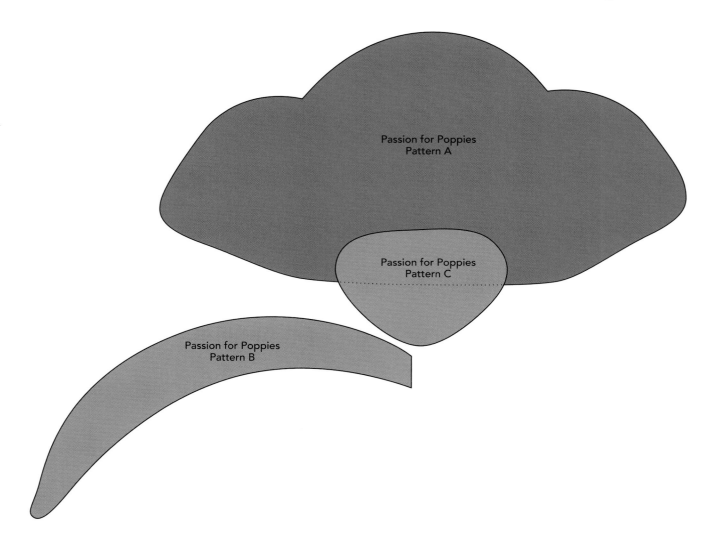

Passion for Poppies
Pattern A

Passion for Poppies
Pattern C

Passion for Poppies
Pattern B

## ASSEMBLE AND ADD THE OUTER BORDER

**1.** Referring to Diagram 10 for placement, sew the four red plaid and one solid red 3½×27" strips into a strip set; press. Cut the strip set into sixteen 1½"-wide segments.

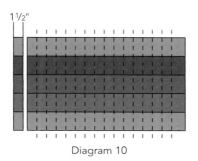

Diagram 10

**2.** Referring to the photograph on *page 36* for placement, offset the rectangles in the 1½"-wide segments to make the outer border. The first row of a side outer border strip begins with eight full-size rectangles, followed by a 2"-long rectangle (see Diagram 11). The second row begins with one 2"-long rectangle, followed by eight full-size rectangles, as shown. Sew the two rows together to make a side outer border strip; press. The pieced side outer border strip should measure 2½×26", including the seam allowances. In the same manner, make a second side outer border strip, reversing the order of the rectangles. Sew the side outer border strips to the side edges of the quilt center. Press the seam allowances in one direction.

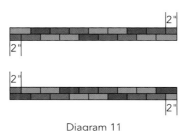

Diagram 11

**3.** The first row of the top outer border strip begins with a 3"-long rectangle, followed by nine full-size rectangles, as shown in Diagram 12. The second row begins with one 1½"-long rectangle, followed by nine full-size rectangles, and ending with one 2"-long rectangle. Join the rows to make a top outer border strip; press the seam allowance in one direction. The pieced top outer border strip should measure 2½×30", including the seam allowances. Make a bottom outer border strip in the same manner. Sew the borders to the top and bottom edges of the quilt center to complete the quilt top. Press the seam allowances in one direction.

Diagram 12

## COMPLETE THE QUILT

**1.** Layer the quilt top, batting, and backing according to the instructions in Quilting Basics, which begins on *page 94.*

**2.** Quilt as desired. Kris used taupe perle cotton No. 8 for a homespun touch. She machine-stitched in the ditch between the strips in the outer border units.

**3.** Use the navy plaid 2½×42" binding strips to bind the quilt according to the instructions in Quilting Basics.

## SPRINGTIME BEAUTY

Looking for a lighter color combination than the original? Use a palette of soft purple and yellow prints for the wall hanging.

# French Toile Medallion

True to the time, hand-stitched embellishments frame a toile print—all, careful replications of yesterday's fabric.

## MATERIALS

¾ yard of solid ivory for appliqué foundation

⅜ yard of red print for sashing and inner border

⅝ yard of red-and-cream toile for middle border

1⅓ yards of red-and-black toile for outer border

½ yard of blue-and-cream toile for center

½ yard of floral chintz for broderie perse appliqués

⅜ yard of navy print for binding

2¼ yards of backing fabric

50×56" of quilt batting

Finished quilt top: 43½×49½"

Quantities specified for 44/45"-wide, 100% cotton fabrics. All measurements include a ¼" seam allowance. Sew with right sides together unless otherwise stated.

Design: Pat L. Nickols
Photograph: Perry Struse

## CUT THE FABRICS

To make the best use of your fabrics cut the pieces in the order that follows. The outer border strips are cut the length of the fabric (parallel to the selvage).

*From solid ivory, cut:*
- 1—23½×29½" appliqué foundation rectangle

*From red print, cut:*
- 2—1¾×29½" inner border strips
- 2—1¾×26" inner border strips
- 4—1¾×14" sashing strips

*From red-and-cream toile, cut:*
- 2—5×35" middle border strips
- 2—5×32" middle border strips

*From red-and-black toile, cut:*
- 2—5×44" outer border strips
- 2—5×41" outer border strips

*From blue-and-cream toile, cut:*
- 1—11½" square

*From navy print, cut:*
- 5—2½×42" binding strips

## ASSEMBLE THE QUILT TOP

**1.** Sew the red print 1¾×29½" inner border strips to long edges of the solid ivory 23½×29½"appliqué foundation. Then add the red print 1¾×26" inner border strips to the short edges of the appliqué foundation to make the quilt center. Press all seam allowances toward the red print border.

**2.** Sew the red-and-cream toile 5×32" middle border strips to the long edges of the quilt center. Then add the red-and-cream toile 5×35" outer border strips to the short edges of the quilt center. Press all seam allowances toward the red-and-cream toile border.

**3.** Sew the red-and-black toile 5×41" outer border strips to long edges of the quilt center. Then add the red-and-black toile 5×44" outer border strips to the short edges of the quilt center to complete the quilt top. Press all seam allowances toward the red-and-black toile border.

## APPLIQUÉ THE QUILT TOP

**1.** Add the red print sashing strips to the blue-and-cream toile 11½" square, mitering the corners, to create the center appliqué square.

**2.** Turn under the raw edges of the center appliqué square ³⁄₁₆"; baste in place.

**3.** Lay the prepared square atop the quilt top's solid ivory appliqué foundation. Pat placed the square approximately 3" from the foundation's top edge, 4" from the foundation's bottom edge, and centered side to side. When pleased with the placement, baste the square in place.

**4.** Using thread in a color that matches the fabric, appliqué the square in place.

**5.** To create the broderie perse appliqués, select small- and large-scale flowers and birds from the floral chintz. Cut out selected motifs, adding a ³⁄₁₆" seam allowance to each.

**6.** Arrange the appliqués atop the quilt top's appliqué foundation. When pleased with the arrangement, baste in place.

**7.** Using threads in colors that match and working from the bottom layer to the top, appliqué each of the pieces in place.

## COMPLETE THE QUILT

**1.** Layer the quilt top, batting, and backing according to the instructions in Quilting Basics, which begins on *page 94*.

**2.** Quilt as desired. Pat chose to hand-quilt her project. While quilts of the early 1800s often were elaborately quilted, Pat decided less was more in this case. "My aim was to have simple quilting that was easy to reproduce," she says, noting that the "wonderful open areas" allow for more extensive quilting.

**3.** Use the navy print 2½×42" strips to bind the quilt according to the instructions in Quilting Basics.

# String of Pearls

This softly traditional look becomes startlingly contemporary when made with a dark background and pearls of contrasting colors.

## MATERIALS

6½ yards of muslin for appliqué foundations and outer border

1⅛ yards of solid blue for inner border and binding

16—6" squares of assorted gold prints for pearl appliqués

15—6" squares of assorted raspberry prints for pearl appliqués

⅞ yard total of assorted green prints for pearl appliqués

1 yard total of assorted bright blue prints for pearl appliqués

6⅛ yards of backing fabric

87×105" of quilt batting

Sheer, featherweight, nonfusible interfacing material

Finished quilt top: 81×99"
Finished block: 16" square

Quantities specified for 44/45"-wide, 100% cotton fabrics. All measurements include a ¼" seam allowance. Sew with right sides together unless otherwise stated.

Design: Jolyn Olson
Photographs: Perry Struse;
    Steve Struse; Marcia Cameron

## DESIGNER NOTES

Quiltmaker Jolyn Olson carefully planned the placement of the raspberry print and gold print pearl appliqués to create four-petal flowers on the quilt top (see the photograph on *page 44*). For the center of each block, she chose four pearl appliqués of the same raspberry print, and for the corners she purposefully placed a different gold print pearl appliqué (see the Quilt Assembly Diagram on *page 45*). When the blocks were joined into the quilt center, her careful placement brought the corner gold print pearls together to form flowers of the same gold prints.

She laid out the remaining pearl appliqués randomly, then looked at the pieced quilt center for quite some time before deciding on a simple blue frame and muslin border.

## CUT THE FABRICS

To make the best use of your fabrics, cut the pieces in the order that follows. The pattern is on *page 46*. To make a template of the pattern, follow the instructions in Appliqué Primer, which begins on *page 2*. The muslin border strips are cut the length of the fabric (parallel to the selvage).

*From muslin, cut:*
- 2—8¾×99½" outer border strips
- 2—8¾×65" outer border strips
- 15—16½" squares for appliqué foundations
- 10—7½×16½" rectangles for appliqué foundations

*From solid blue, cut:*
- 9—2½×42" binding strips
- 7—1¾×42" strips for inner border

## PREPARE THE APPLIQUÉS

To use double-appliqué method for appliquéing, as was done in this project, complete the following steps.

**1.** Trace the template four times on the wrong side of each gold print and raspberry print 6" square, leaving ½" between tracings. The traced line is your stitching line.

**2.** Layer each marked fabric square right side down on a like-size piece of nonfusible interfacing. Using thread that matches the fabric, stitch on the drawn lines, beginning

# String of Pearls

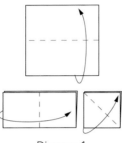

rectangle in half, making a square. Then fold each square in half diagonally, bringing together the folded edges, to make a triangle. Press the folded edges well to ensure precise placement lines. Unfold the squares.

Diagram 1

Fold each muslin 7½×16½" rectangle in half to make a square (see Diagram 2). Then fold each square in half diagonally to make a triangle. Press the folded edges well. Unfold the rectangles.

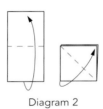

Diagram 2

**2.** Referring to Diagram 3 for placement, arrange four raspberry print pearl appliqués, 12 bright blue print pearl appliqués, and four gold print pearl appliqués on a creased muslin 16½" square appliqué foundation. Add four green print pearl appliqués, placing their points 1¼" from the center of the raspberry flower. Be sure to allow for a ¼" seam allowance around the edge of the block. You may wish to mark the seam line on the foundation to aid in placement. When pleased with the arrangement, baste the pieces in place.

and ending the stitching on the sides of the pearls. Do not start stitching at a point.

**3.** Trim each pearl appliqué shape to ⅛" beyond the stitching. Make a slit in the center of each interfacing shape, being careful not to cut through the attached fabric shape. Carefully turn each stitched shape right side out, pushing out the points, to make a total of 64 gold print and 60 raspberry print pearl appliqués for the flowers. Finger-press the seam allowances.

**4.** Repeat steps 1 through 3 to make 124 green print pearl appliqués for the leaves and 144 bright blue print pearl appliqués for the connecting strings.

## APPLIQUÉ THE BLOCKS
**1.** Fold each muslin 16½" square in half horizontally, making a rectangle (see Diagram 1). Fold each

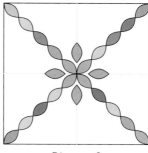

Diagram 3

**3.** Using threads in colors that match the pearls, stitch the pearl appliqués to the foundation.

**4.** Repeat steps 2 and 3 to appliqué a total of nine blocks.

**5.** In the same manner, appliqué the creased muslin foundations as follows: six 16½" squares as shown in Diagram 4, six 7½×16½" rectangles as shown in Diagram 5, two 7½×16½" rectangles as shown in Diagram 6, and two 7½×16½" rectangles as shown in Diagram 7.

## ASSEMBLE THE QUILT CENTER

**1.** Referring to the Quilt Assembly Diagram for placement, lay out all the appliquéd blocks in five horizontal rows, carefully noting the placement of the appliquéd gold pearls so the fabrics match.

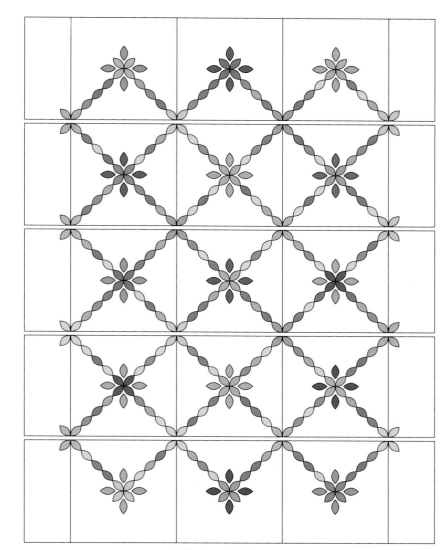

Quilt Assembly Diagram

Diagram 4

Diagram 5

Diagram 6

Diagram 7

# String of Pearls

**2.** Sew together the blocks in each row. Press the seam allowances open. Then join the rows to make the quilt center. Press the seam allowances open. The pieced quilt center should measure 62½×80½", including the seam allowances.

**3.** As was done in the block centers, place four green print pearl appliqués around each of the gold print flowers, placing them on the seams, with points 1¼" from the flower centers (see the photograph on *page 44* for placement).

**4.** Using thread that matches the pearls, appliqué the pieces in place.

## ADD THE BORDERS

**1.** Cut and piece the solid blue 1¾×42" strips to make the following:
- 2—1¾×83" inner border strips
- 2—1¾×62½" inner border strips

**2.** Sew the short solid blue inner border strips to the short edges of the appliquéd quilt center. Then join the long solid blue inner border strips to the long edges of the quilt center. Press all seam allowances toward the inner border.

**3.** Sew the muslin 8¾×65" outer border strips to the short edges of the quilt center. Then join the muslin 8¾×99½" outer border strips

to the long edges of the quilt center to complete the quilt top. Press all seam allowances toward the inner border.

## COMPLETE THE QUILT

**1.** Layer the quilt top, batting, and backing according to the instructions in Quilting Basics, which begins on *page 94*.

**2.** Quilt as desired. Jolyn hand-quilted this project using a purchased stencil.

**3.** Use the solid blue 2½×42" strips to bind the quilt according to the instructions in Quilting Basics.

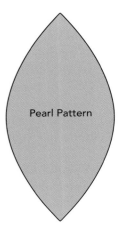

Pearl Pattern

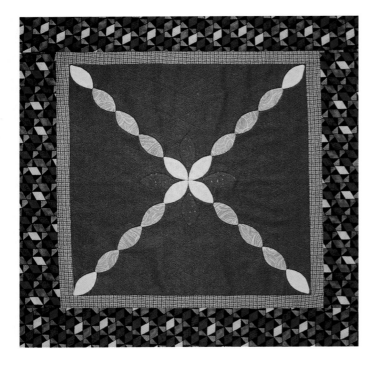

## STRINGING IT TOGETHER

A solid blue background changes the overall look of this project dramatically. The bright multicolor border pulls together all of the colors used in the appliqués.

# Today's Appliqué:
# Fused and Hand Stitched

The projects in this section are simply deceiving—they're much easier than they look! Use fusible web to iron a shape onto a quilt top, then hand-stitch around it.

An uneven blanket stitch distinguishes hand-made gifts from manufacturer replications—so even beginners can quickly create extraordinary art.

This simple technique employs today's materials. The results, as you see, are a clear reflection of style, personality, and the times of our lives!

Embellish a Log Cabin block with leaves and acorns
for a pillow that is as comforting as a warm autumn fire.

# Split Oak Leaf Pillows

## MATERIALS FOR ONE PILLOW

1⅔ yards of chestnut-and-black large check for center square, binding, and pillow back

⅜ yard total of assorted gold prints for Log Cabin blocks

⅜ yard total of assorted red prints for Log Cabin blocks

¼ yard of green print for leaf appliqués

⅛ yard of chestnut-and-black small check for circle appliqués

½ yard of lightweight fusible web

Black embroidery floss

24" square of muslin for lining

24" square of polyester batting

20" square pillow form

Finished pillow top: 20⅝" square

Quantities specified for 44/45" wide, 100% cotton fabrics. All measurements include a ¼" seam allowance. Sew with right sides together unless otherwise stated.

Design: Lynette Jensen
Photographs: Hopkins Associates

## CUT THE FABRICS

To make the best use of your fabrics, cut the pieces in the order that follows. The patterns are on *page 51.* To use fusible web for appliquéing, as was done in this project, complete the following steps.

**1.** Lay the fusible web, paper side up, over the patterns. Use a pencil to trace each pattern the number of times indicated, leaving a ½" space between tracings. Cut out each piece roughly ¼" outside the traced lines.

**2.** Following the manufacturer's instructions, press the fusible-web shapes onto the wrong sides of the designated fabrics; let cool. Cut out the fabric shapes on the drawn lines. Peel off the paper backing.

*From chestnut-and-black large check, cut:*
- 2—21½×24" pieces for pillow back
- 1—18×42" rectangle, cutting it into enough 6¼"-wide bias strips to total 105" in length (For specific instructions, see Cutting Bias Strips in Appliqué Primer, which begins on *page 2.*)
- 1—3½" square for center

*From assorted gold prints, cut:*
- 1—3½×18½" rectangle for position 14
- 1—3½×15½" rectangle for position 13
- 1—2½×13½" rectangle for position 10
- 1—2½×11½" rectangle for position 9
- 1—2½×9½" rectangle for position 6
- 1—2½×7½" rectangle for position 5
- 1—2½×5½" rectangle for position 2
- 1—2½×3½" rectangle for position 1

*From assorted red prints, cut:*
- 1—3½×21½" rectangle for position 16
- 1—3½×18½" rectangle for position 15
- 1—2½×15½" rectangle for position 12
- 1—2½×13½" rectangle for position 11
- 1—2½×11½" rectangle for position 8
- 1—2½×9½" rectangle for position 7

- 1—2½×7½" rectangle for position 4
- 1—2½×5½" rectangle for position 3

*From green print, cut:*
- 4 of Pattern A

*From chestnut-and-black small check, cut:*
- 12 of Pattern B

## ASSEMBLE THE LOG CABIN BLOCK

**1.** Sew the gold print position 1 rectangle to the top of the chestnut-and-black large check 3½" center square to create the center block (see Diagram 1). Press the seam allowance toward the center square.

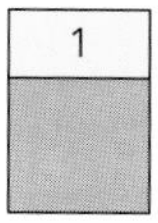

Diagram 1

**2.** Referring to Diagram 2 for placement, sew the light gold print position 2 rectangle to the left side of the center block. Press the seam allowance toward the center block.

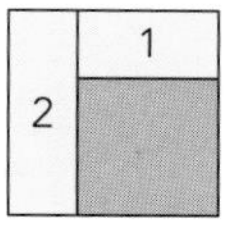

Diagram 2

**3.** Add the red print position 3 rectangle to the bottom edge. Press the seam allowance toward the center block. Continue sewing the pieces to the center block in a counterclockwise direction, following the numerical sequence shown in Diagram 3 on *page 50,* until you've completed the log cabin block. Press all seam allowances toward the center block. The pieced Log Cabin block should measure 21½" square, including the seam allowances.

# Split Oak Leaf Pillows

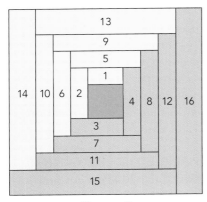

Diagram 3

## MAKE THE PILLOW TOP

**1.** Referring to the photograph on *page 48* for placement, place the oak leaf and circle appliqués on the pieced Log Cabin block; fuse in place with a hot, dry iron. Let the fabrics cool.

**2.** Using the blanket stitch and three strands of black embroidery floss, appliqué the leaves and circles in place to complete the pillow top. (For instructions on the blanket stitch, see Appliqué Primer, which begins on *page 2*.)

## QUILT THE PILLOW TOP

**1.** Layer the pillow top, batting, and muslin lining according to the instructions in Quilting Basics, which begins on *page 94*.

**2.** Quilt as desired. Lynette hand-quilted in the ditch along the Log Cabin seam lines and around each oak leaf and circle; trim excess batting and muslin.

## MAKE THE PILLOW BACK

**1.** With wrong sides together, fold the two chestnut-and-black large check 21½×24" pillow back pieces in half to form two double-thick 12×21½" pieces. Overlap the folded edges by 2".

**2.** Stitch across the folds ½" from the top and bottom edges to secure the back pieces. The double thickness makes the pillow back more stable and finishes it nicely.

## COMPLETE THE PILLOW

**1.** With wrong sides together, layer the pillow top and the pillow back. Using a ¾" seam allowance, sew the pieces together along all four edges.

**2.** Use the chestnut-and-black large check 6¼"-wide bias strips and a ⅞-wide seam allowance to bind the quilt according to the instructions in Quilting Basics.

**3.** Insert a pillow form through the back opening.

### BRILLIANT FALL COLORS

Instead of making pillows, stitch four Log Cabin blocks together and create a 39½" square wall hanging.

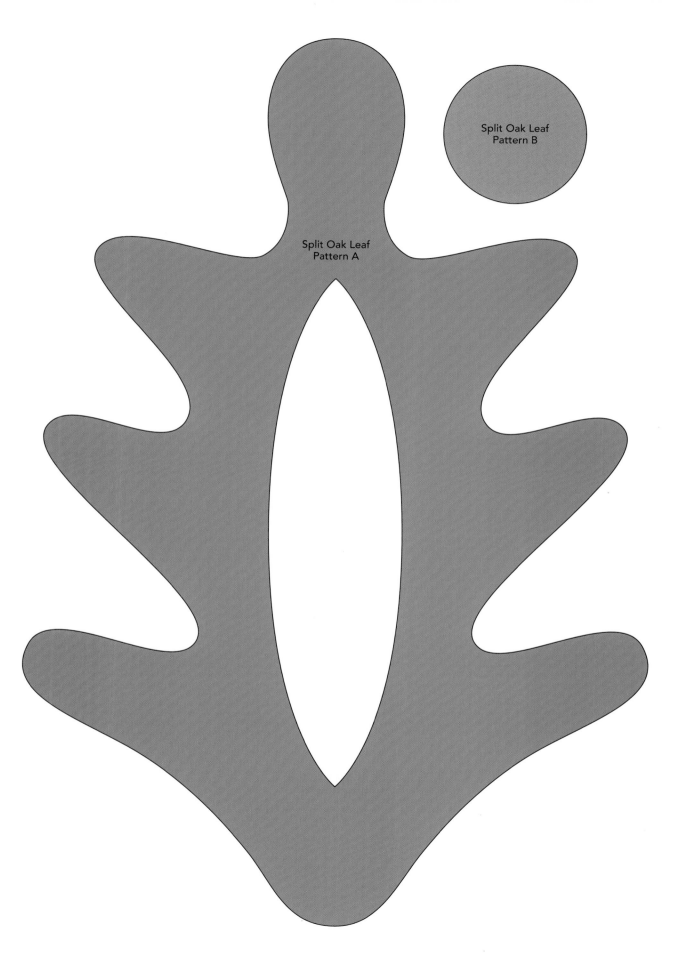

Split Oak Leaf
Pattern B

Split Oak Leaf
Pattern A

The gentle colors of spring flowers and simple, angular quilting: This is a beautiful way to share sunshine in all weather.

# Meadow Blooms

## MATERIALS

¼ yard of off-white print for appliqué foundations

¼ yard of yellow print for setting squares and triangles

⅜ yard of green print No. 1 for inner border and binding

¼ yard of green print No. 2 for vine and stem appliqués

½ yard of cream print for outer border

Scraps of assorted pink, purple, yellow, and green prints for flower and leaf appliqués

1 yard of backing fabric

29×35" of quilt batting

1½ yards of lightweight fusible web

Embroidery floss in colors to match appliqués

23—½"-diameter yellow buttons for flower centers

Finished quilt top: 23½×28⅞"
Finished blocks: 4" square

Quantities specified for 44/45"-wide, 100% cotton fabrics. All measurements include a ¼" seam allowance. Sew with right sides together unless otherwise stated.

Design: Cynthia Tomaszewski
Photographs: Marcia Cameron

## CUT THE FABRICS

To make the best use of your fabrics, cut the pieces in the order that follows. The patterns are on pages 56–57.

To use fusible web for appliquéing, as was done in this project, complete the following steps.

**1.** Lay the fusible web, paper side up, over the patterns. Use a pencil to trace each pattern the number of times indicated below, leaving a ½" space between tracings. Cut out each piece roughly ¼" outside the traced lines.

**2.** Following the manufacturer's instructions, press the fusible-web shapes onto the wrong side of the designated fabrics; let cool. Cut out the fabric shapes on the drawn lines. Peel off the paper backing.

*From off-white print, cut:*
- 6—4½" squares

*From yellow print, cut:*
- 2—7" squares, cutting each diagonally twice in an X for a total of 8 setting triangles (you'll have 2 leftover)
- 2—4½" squares for setting squares

- 2—3¾" squares, cutting each in half diagonally for a total of 4 corner triangles

*From green print No. 1, cut:*
- 3—2½×42" binding strips
- 2—1½×19⅜" inner border strips
- 2—1½×11¾" inner border strips

*From green print No. 2, cut:*
- 1—9" square, cutting it into enough ½"-wide bias strips to total 130" in length for stems and vines (For specific instructions, see Cutting Bias Strips in Appliqué Primer, which begins on *page 2.*)

*From cream print, cut:*
- 2—5½×29⅜" outer border strips
- 2—5½×13¾" outer border strips

*From assorted pink prints, cut:*
- 10 of Pattern H
- 9 of Pattern P
- 4 of Pattern O
- 1 *each* of patterns A, B, K, and L

*From assorted purple prints, cut:*
- 6 of Pattern P
- 3 *each* of patterns E and F
- 1 of Pattern H

*From assorted yellow prints, cut:*
- 7 of Pattern H
- 3 of Pattern G

*From assorted green prints, cut:*
- 45 of Pattern Q
- 1 *each* of patterns C, D, I, J, M, and N

# Meadow Blooms

## APPLIQUÉ THE BLOCKS

**1.** Referring to the photograph *above* and the full-size appliqué patterns on *pages 56–57,* lay out the flower and leaf appliqués on the six off-white print 4½" square appliqué foundations. Cut the green print No. 2 bias strip into stems as needed.

**2.** Turning under a ⅛" seam allowance, slip-stitch the stems in place with green thread.

**3.** Reposition and iron each flower and leaf appliqué piece in place.

**4.** Using a single strand of a matching embroidery floss, blanket-stitch around each appliqué flower and leaf. (For instructions on the blanket stitch, see Appliqué Primer, which begins on *page 2.*)

**5.** Using one strand of green embroidery floss, stem-stitch vine tendrils on the flower block as

indicated on the full-size appliqué patterns. (For instructions on the stem stitch, see Appliqué Primer, which begins on *page 2.*)

## ASSEMBLE THE QUILT CENTER

**1.** Referring to the Quilt Assembly Diagram for placement, lay out the six appliquéd blocks, the two yellow print 4½" setting squares, the six yellow print setting triangles, and the four yellow print corner triangles in diagonal rows.

Quilt Assembly Diagram

**2.** Sew together the pieces in each diagonal row. Press the seam allowances toward the setting squares and triangles. Then join the rows to make the quilt center, adding the four yellow print corner triangles last. Press the seam allowances in one direction. The pieced quilt center should measure $11\frac{3}{4} \times 17\frac{3}{8}$", including the seam allowances.

### ADD THE BORDERS

**1.** Sew the green print $1\frac{1}{2} \times 11\frac{3}{4}$" inner border strips to the top and bottom edges of the pieced quilt center. Sew the green print $1\frac{1}{2} \times 19\frac{3}{8}$" inner border strips to the side edges of the pieced quilt center. Press all seam allowances toward the inner border.

**2.** Sew the cream print $5\frac{1}{2} \times 13\frac{3}{4}$" outer border strips to the top and bottom edges of the pieced quilt center. Sew the cream print $5\frac{1}{2} \times 29\frac{3}{8}$" outer border strips to the side edges of the pieced quilt center

to complete the quilt top. Press all seam allowances toward the outer border.

### APPLIQUÉ THE BORDER

**1.** Referring to the photograph *opposite* for placement, lay out the remaining green print bias strip as a vine on the cream print outer border. Turning under a $\frac{1}{8}$" seam allowance, use small slip stitches and green thread to stitch the vine in place.

**2.** Lay out the remaining flower and leaf appliqués; fuse in place.

**3.** Using a single strand of matching embroidery floss, blanket-stitch around each flower and leaf appliqué.

### COMPLETE THE QUILT

**1.** Layer the quilt top, batting, and backing according to the

instructions in Quilting Basics, which begins on *page 94*.

**2.** Quilt as desired. Cynthia hand-quilted a 1" crosshatch grid on the diagonal.

**3.** With embroidery floss, sew a button on each flower center, tying the thread tails on top of the button.

To tie the button on, first push the needle down through the buttonhole, leaving a 3" thread tail. Bring the needle back up through the opposite buttonhole and cut the thread 3" above the button. Tie the thread tails in a knot to secure the button to the quilt top. Trim the thread tails to $\frac{1}{4}$".

**4.** Use the green print $2\frac{1}{2} \times 42$" strips to bind the quilt according to the instructions in Quilting Basics.

### FRAME IT UP

Choose a darker color palette to re-create this project in a horizontal setting. Its smaller size is perfect for framing.

# Meadow Blooms

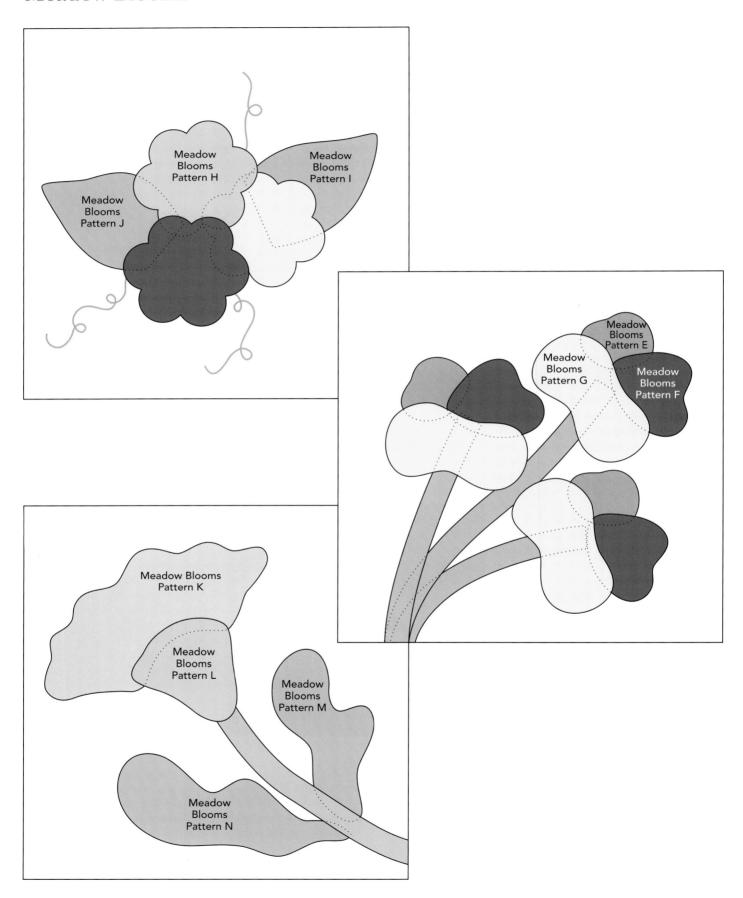

Meadow Blooms Pattern H

Meadow Blooms Pattern I

Meadow Blooms Pattern J

Meadow Blooms Pattern E

Meadow Blooms Pattern G

Meadow Blooms Pattern F

Meadow Blooms Pattern K

Meadow Blooms Pattern L

Meadow Blooms Pattern M

Meadow Blooms Pattern N

Meadow
Blooms
Pattern O

Meadow
Blooms
Pattern Q

Meadow
Blooms
Pattern P

Meadow
Blooms
Pattern H

Meadow Blooms
Pattern A

Meadow
Blooms
Pattern C

Meadow
Blooms
Pattern B

Meadow
Blooms
Pattern D

On a whim, you can convert this delectable place mat into a table quilt or wall hanging—it's much easier to grow than a garden.

# Vegetable Garden

## MATERIALS

18×22" piece (fat quarter) of solid off-white for appliqué foundation

Scraps of assorted green plaids for carrot top, pea pod and peas, bell pepper and stem, tomato stem, and beet stem appliqués

2—6" squares of assorted red plaids for tomato and beet appliqués

3×7" rectangle of orange plaid for carrot appliqué

⅝ yard of red-and-black plaid for border, binding, and backing

24×18" of quilt batting

¾ yard of lightweight fusible web

Black embroidery floss

Finished quilt top: 17¾×12½"

Quantities specified for 44/45"-wide, 100% cotton fabrics. All measurements include a ¼" seam allowance. Sew with right sides together unless otherwise stated.

Design: Laurene Sinema
Photographs: Perry Struse;
    Marcia Cameron

## CUT THE FABRICS

To make the best use of your fabrics, cut the pieces in the order that follows. The patterns are on *pages 60–61*.

To use fusible web for appliquéing, as was done in this project, complete the following steps.

**1.** Lay the fusible web, paper side up, over the patterns. Use a pencil to trace each pattern the number of times indicated, leaving a ½" space between tracings. Cut out each piece roughly ¼" outside the traced lines.

**2.** Following the manufacturer's instructions, press the fusible web shapes onto the wrong sides of the designated fabrics; let cool. Cut out the fabric shapes on the drawn lines. Peel off the paper backing.

*From solid off-white, cut:*
- 1—5½×10" rectangle (carrot appliqué foundation)
- 2—5½×5¼" rectangles (pea and bell pepper appliqué foundations)
- 1—5¼×6¼" rectangle (beet appliqué foundation)

- 1—5¼×4¼" rectangle (tomato appliqué foundation)

*From assorted green plaids, cut:*
- 1 *each* of patterns A, B, C, D, E, G, H, I, and J
- 6 of Pattern F

*From assorted red plaids, cut:*
- 1 *each* of patterns K and L

*From orange plaid, cut:*
- 1 of Pattern M

*From red-and-black plaid, cut:*
- 1—18×24" rectangle for backing
- 1—14" square, cutting it into enough 2½"-wide bias strips to total 70" in length for binding (For specific instructions, see Cutting Bias Strips in Appliqué Primer, which begins on *page 2*.)
- 2—2×15¼" border strips
- 2—2×13" border strips

## APPLIQUÉ THE BLOCKS

**1.** Referring to the photograph *opposite*, center the appliqué pieces on the corresponding off-white rectangles. Fuse the appliqués in place.

**2.** Using two strands of black embroidery floss, stitch a running

# Vegetable Garden

stitch around each appliqué piece. On the very narrow stems, stitch down the center as shown on the pattern pieces. The peas are only stitched with a cross-stitch in the center. The pea tendrils are stitched with a running stitch. (For instructions on the running stitch and the cross-stitch, see Appliqué Primer, which begins on *page 2*.)

### ASSEMBLE THE QUILT CENTER

**1.** Referring to the photograph on *page 58*, lay out the five appliqué blocks in three vertical rows.

**2.** Sew together the blocks in each row and press the seam allowances in one direction. Then join the rows to make the quilt center; press the seam allowances in one direction. The pieced quilt center should measure 15¼×10", including the seam allowances.

### ADD THE BORDER

**1.** Sew the red-and-black plaid 2×15¼" border strips to the top and bottom edges of the pieced quilt center. Press the seam allowances toward the border.

**2.** Then add the red-and-black plaid 2×13" border strips to the side edges of the pieced quilt center to complete the quilt top. Press the seam allowances toward the border.

### COMPLETE THE QUILT

**1.** Layer the quilt top, batting, and backing according to the instructions in Quilting Basics, which begins on *page 94*.

**2.** Quilt as desired. Laurene machine-stitched in the ditch around each block and appliqué shape.

**3.** Use the red-and-black plaid 2½"-wide bias strips to bind the quilt according to the instructions in Quilting Basics.

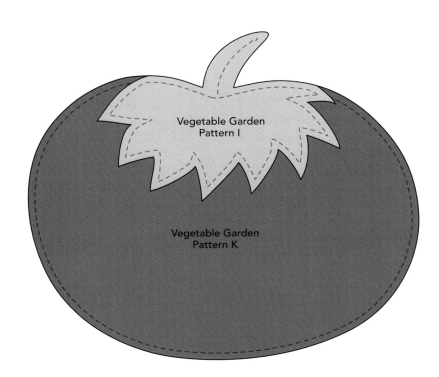

Vegetable Garden Pattern I

Vegetable Garden Pattern K

### THREE PEAS IN A POD

For a whimsical gardener's notebook, fuse three pea pods on a 3-ring binder, then hot-glue buttons in place for peas. Use a fine black marker to draw dashed lines for tendrils.

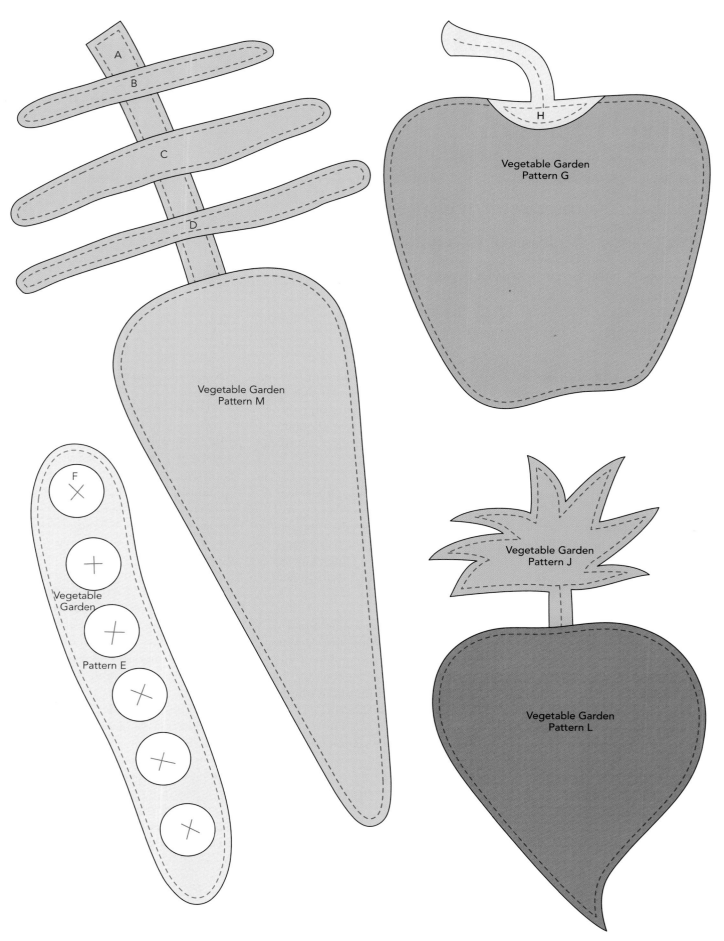

A

B

C

D

Vegetable Garden
Pattern M

Vegetable Garden
Pattern G

H

F

Vegetable
Garden

Pattern E

Vegetable Garden
Pattern J

Vegetable Garden
Pattern L

# Sun Dance

Celebrate autumn's warm glow—or, with a change in color palette, spring's eager start—with this surprisingly simple showpiece.

## MATERIALS

- 9—18×22" pieces (fat quarters) of assorted green, tan, gold, brown, and gray wool plaids for appliqué foundations and pieced border
- 18—9×22" pieces (fat eighths) of assorted solid yellow, green, pink, gold, brown, rust, red, gray, and blue wools for sun appliqués and pieced border
- ¼ yard of rust wool for binding
- 2⅞ yards of cotton backing fabric
- 1 yard of lightweight fusible web
- 6 skeins of tan embroidery floss for appliqués and quilting

Finished quilt top: 46" square
Finished block: 12" square

Quantities specified for 44/45"-wide, 100% wool and 100% cotton fabrics. All measurements include a ¼" seam allowance. Sew with right sides together unless otherwise stated.

Design: Jill Kemp
Photographs: Perry Struse;
    Marcia Cameron

## CUT THE FABRICS

To make the best use of your fabrics, cut the pieces in the order that follows. The patterns are on *page 65*. To use fusible web for appliquéing, as was done in this project, complete the following steps.

**1.** Lay the fusible web, paper side up, over the patterns. Use a pencil to trace each pattern the number of times indicated below, leaving a ½" space between tracings. Cut out each piece roughly ¼" outside the traced lines.

**2.** Following the manufacturer's instructions, press the fusible-web shapes onto the wrong side of the designated fabrics; let cool. Cut out the fabric shapes on the drawn lines. Peel off the paper backing.

*From each of the 9 assorted wool plaids, cut:*
- 1—13" square

*From 9 of the assorted wool solids, cut:*
- 9 of Pattern A

*From each of the 9 remaining assorted wool solids, cut:*
- 12 of Pattern B

*From solid rust wool, cut:*
- 5—1½×42" binding strips

## APPLIQUÉ THE BLOCKS

**1.** Referring to the photograph on *page 64* for placement, place one Pattern A circle and 12 Pattern B points on each wool plaid 13" square appliqué foundation, tucking the wide end of each point ¼" under the circles. When the appliqué pieces are in the correct position, fuse them in place.

*Note:* It takes a little more time to fuse wool than it does to fuse cotton fabric. Before you begin, test your iron to see how long it takes for the fusible web to adhere one wool scrap to another. Designer Jill Kemp says her iron takes about 15 seconds.

**2.** Using three strands of gray embroidery floss, blanket-stitch the appliqués in place. (For instructions on the blanket stitch, see Appliqué Primer, which begins on *page 2*.)

**3.** Press and trim each appliquéd block to measure 12½" square, including the seam allowances.

# Sun Dance

## ASSEMBLE THE QUILT CENTER

**1.** Lay out the nine appliquéd wool blocks in three horizontal rows.

**2.** Sew together the blocks in each row. Press the seam allowances open. Then join the rows to complete the quilt center. Press the seam allowances open. The pieced quilt center should measure 36½" square, including the seam allowances.

## ADD THE BORDER

**1.** Cut and piece the remaining assorted wool scraps to make the following:
- 2—5½×46½" border strips
- 2—5½×36½" border strips

**2.** Sew the short border strips to opposite edges of the pieced quilt center. Then add the long border strips to the remaining edges of the pieced quilt center to complete the quilt top. Press the seam allowances toward the pieced wool border.

## COMPLETE THE QUILT

**1.** Layer the quilt top and backing with wrong sides together. Quilt as desired. Jill used three strands of gray embroidery floss and long stitches to hand-quilt this project. She outlined each sun and stitched about ¼" on each side of the border seams.

**2.** Cut and piece the solid rust 1½×42" strips to make the following:
- 4—1½×46½" strips

**3.** Fold the wool binding strip in half lengthwise with the wrong sides inside; press. Position a binding strip over the edge of the quilt. Using three strands of gray embroidery floss, stitch the strip in place. Repeat with the remaining folded and pressed binding strips to bind the quilt.

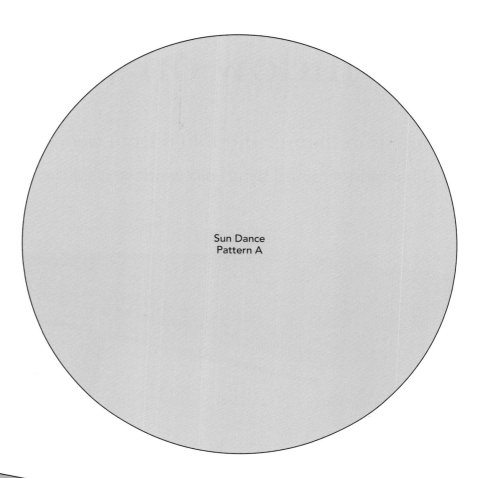

Sun Dance
Pattern A

Sun Dance
Pattern B

## NIGHT GLOW

Black-and-tan plaid and homespuns are the backdrop to yellow fused and machine-appliquéd stars.

# A Window on the Seasons

Homespun flannel and felted wool team up for this all-season
wall hanging. Framed by an old window, it's a decorator's delight.

## MATERIALS

½ yard of beige plaid for appliqué foundations

18×22" piece (fat quarter) of tan plaid No. 1 for appliqué foundations

18×22" piece (fat quarter) of tan plaid No. 2 for appliqué foundations

4×6" piece of felted purple wool for appliqués

8" square of green plaid for appliqués

8" square of red plaid for appliqués

3½×7" square of orange plaid for appliqué

3" square of felted brown wool for appliqué

2½" square of felted brown tweed wool for appliqué

3×9" piece of felted dark blue wool for appliqué

6×8" piece of felted red wool for appliqué

8" square of felted green wool for appliqués

⅜ yard of backing fabric

Window frame with four 10×12" openings

4—10×12" pieces of mat board

3—1¾"-diameter ceramic star buttons

3—¾"-diameter red buttons

Embroidery floss: red, blue, tan, brown, and green

1 yard of lightweight fusible web

Finished block: 11×13"

Quantities specified for 44/45"-wide, 100% cotton fabrics. All measurements include a ¼" seam allowance. Sew with right sides together unless otherwise stated.

Design: Lynne Hagmeier
Photographs: Perry Struse;
    Craig Anderson

## CUT THE FABRICS

To make the best use of your fabrics, cut the pieces in the order that follows in each section. The patterns are on *page 70*. To use fusible web for appliquéing, as was done in this project, complete the following steps.

**1.** Lay the fusible web, paper side up, over the patterns. With a pencil, trace each pattern the number of times indicated, leaving ½" between tracings. Cut out the pieces roughly ¼" outside the traced lines.

**2.** Following the manufacturer's instructions, press the fusible-web shapes onto the back of the designated fabrics; let cool. Cut out the shapes on the drawn lines. Peel off the paper backing.

*From beige plaid, cut:*
- 1—14½" square, cutting it in half diagonally for a total of 2 triangles (You'll have 1 leftover.)
- 1—5×13½" rectangle
- 2—6×7" rectangles
- 1—5½×7½" rectangle
- 4—3½" squares

*From tan plaid No. 1, cut:*
- 1—3¾×13½" rectangle
- 1—6×7" rectangle
- 2—3½×7½" rectangles
- 2—3½×5½" rectangles

*From tan plaid No. 2, cut:*
- 1—14½" square, cutting it in half diagonally for a total of 2 triangles (You'll have 1 leftover.)
- 1—6×7" rectangle (Cut from the leftover triangle fabric.)
- 1—3¾×13½" rectangle

*From purple wool, cut:*
- 1 each of patterns A and B

*From green plaid, cut:*
- 1 *each* of patterns C, D, E, F, F reversed, and G

*From red plaid, cut:*
- 2 of Pattern H

*From orange plaid, cut:*
- 1 of Pattern G

*From brown wool, cut:*
- 1 of Pattern J

*From brown tweed wool, cut:*
- 1 of Pattern I

*From dark blue wool, cut:*
- 1—2¼×7¾" rectangle

*From red wool, cut:*
- 3 of Pattern K

*From green wool, cut:*
- 2 of Pattern L

*From fused backing fabric, cut:*
- 4—10×12" rectangles

## ASSEMBLE THE APPLIQUÉ FOUNDATIONS

**1.** Referring to Diagram 1 for placement, lay out the four beige plaid 3½" squares, the beige plaid 5½×7½" rectangle, the two tan plaid No. 1 3½×7½" rectangles, and the two tan plaid No. 1 3½×5½" rectangles in three vertical rows. Sew together the pieces in each row. Press the seam allowances toward the tan plaid pieces. Then join the rows to make the Nine-Patch appliqué foundation. Press the seam allowances in one direction. The pieced foundation should measure 11½×13½", including the seam allowances.

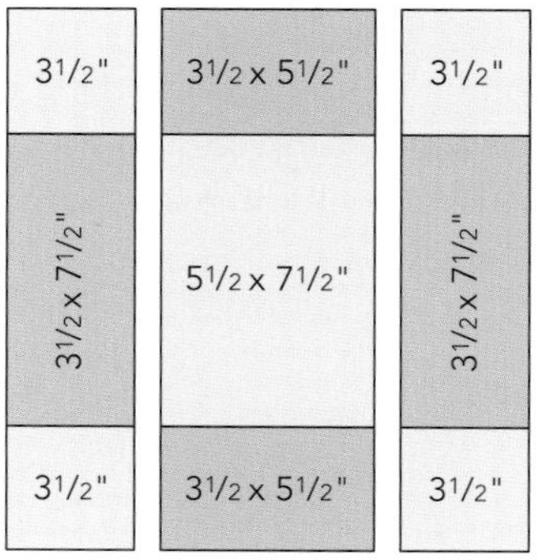

Diagram 1

# A Window on the Seasons

**2.** Referring to Diagram 2 for placement, sew the tan plaid No. 1 and No. 2 3¾×13½" rectangles to opposite long edges of the beige plaid 5×13½" rectangle to make the strip appliqué foundation. Press the seam allowances toward the tan plaid rectangles. The pieced foundation should measure 11½×13½", including the seam allowances.

Diagram 2

**3.** Referring to Diagram 3 for placement, sew together a beige plaid 6×7" rectangle and the tan plaid No. 1 6×7" rectangle to make a pair. Press the seam allowance toward the tan plaid rectangle. Repeat with the remaining beige plaid rectangle and the tan plaid No. 2 6×7" rectangle to make a second pair. Sew together the two pairs to make the Four-Patch appliqué foundation. Press the seam allowance in one direction. The pieced foundation should measure 11½×13½", including the seam allowances.

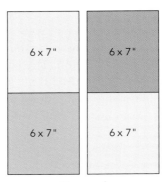

Diagram 3

**4.** Referring to Diagram 4 for placement, sew together one beige plaid triangle and one tan plaid No. 2 triangle to make a triangle unit.

Center and trim the unit to measure 11½×13½", including the seam allowances, to make the triangle appliqué foundation.

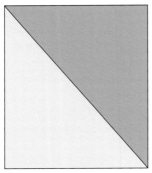

Diagram 4

Appliqué Placement Diagram

## APPLIQUÉ THE BLOCKS

**1.** Referring to the Appliqué Placement Diagram, arrange the tulip, leaf, and stem appliqué pieces on the Nine-Patch foundation. Fuse the appliqués in place. Using threads in colors that match the fabrics, machine-blanket-stitch the pieces in place.

**2.** Arrange the oak leaf and acorn appliqué pieces on the Four-Patch foundation. Fuse the appliqués in place.

Using tan thread, machine-blanket-stitch the edges of the leaves. Using two strands of tan embroidery floss, blanket-stitch the edges of the acorn nut and herringbone-stitch across the acorn cap. (For instructions on the blanket stitch and herringbone stitch, see Appliqué Primer, which begins on *page 2*.)

**3.** Slightly round the corners of the dark blue wool 2¼×7¾" rectangle. Arrange the dark blue wool rectangle and red stripe appliqué pieces on the strip foundation. Fuse the appliqués in place.

Using two strands of red embroidery floss, stitch the stripes with a running stitch. (For instructions on the running stitch, see Appliqué Primer.)

Using two strands of blue embroidery floss, blanket-stitch the edges of the dark blue rectangle. Stitch the star buttons to the block.

Using two strands of brown embroidery floss, satin-stitch a small stem at the top of the acorn cap. (For instructions on the satin stitch, see Appliqué Primer.)

**4.** Arrange the holly leaf appliqué pieces on the triangle appliqué foundation. Fuse the appliqués in place. Using two strands of green embroidery floss, backstitch the leaf veins. Stitch the red buttons to the block. (For instructions on the backstitch, see Appliqué Primer.)

## COMPLETE THE FRAMED WALL HANGING

**1.** Center each completed block on a 10×12" mat board; secure the raw edges to the back with tape. Fuse a backing fabric 10×12" rectangle to the reverse side of each mat board, covering the raw edges.

**2.** Place the four panels in the window frame openings; secure with small nails. Hang as desired.

**YEAR ROUND SAMPLER**

For a more contemporary look, choose cotton fabrics in the colors of the seasons for a wall hanging. Frame each section with a finished 1"-wide sashing before stitching them together.

# A Window on the Seasons

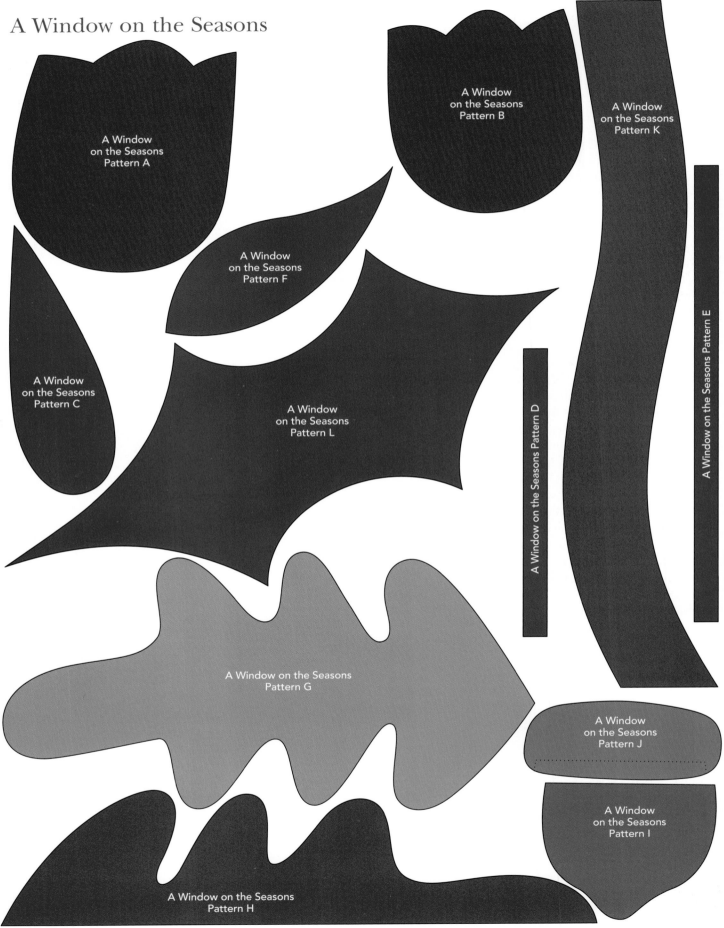

A Window on the Seasons Pattern A

A Window on the Seasons Pattern B

A Window on the Seasons Pattern K

A Window on the Seasons Pattern F

A Window on the Seasons Pattern C

A Window on the Seasons Pattern L

A Window on the Seasons Pattern D

A Window on the Seasons Pattern E

A Window on the Seasons Pattern G

A Window on the Seasons Pattern J

A Window on the Seasons Pattern I

A Window on the Seasons Pattern H

# Fast Art:
# Fused and Machine Stitched

If you're looking for a quick, easy project or a speedier way to appliqué lots of pieces, this is the technique for you. It's handmade with 21st century technology!

Fusible web affixes precut shapes so they "stay put" for the twists and turns of machine sewing. They are sturdy enough to survive everyday use for a long time.

This technique is ideal for hard-to-manage pieces such as sweatshirts and queen-size quilts. It is an opportunity to relish traditional arts even amid a whirlwind of activity.

Atop a gentle white base and framed with a promising print, appliqué tulips warm the winter and inspire spring.

# Promise of Spring

## MATERIALS
¾ yard of tan print for backgrounds
2¼ yards of cranberry print for blocks, tulips, accent border, and binding
3⅝ yards of dark blue print for blocks and borders
¾ yard of mauve print for blocks and tulips
1⅛ yards of green print for blocks, stems, and leaves
3¾ yards of backing fabric
66×82" of quilt batting
Lightweight fusible web
Black sewing thread

Finished quilt top: 59×75¾"
Finished block: 12" square

Quantities specified for 44/45"-wide, 100% cotton fabrics. All measurements include a ¼" seam allowance. Sew with right sides together unless otherwise stated.

Design: Denise Ameen
Photographs: Perry Struse;
  Marcia Cameron

## CUT THE FABRICS
To make the best use of your fabrics, cut the pieces in the order that follows. Cut the border strips the length of the fabric (parallel to the selvage). The patterns are on *pages 76–77.* To use fusible web for appliquéing, as was done in this project, complete the following steps.

**1.** Lay the fusible web, paper side up, over the patterns. Use a pencil to trace each pattern the number of times indicated, leaving a ½" space between tracings. Cut out each piece roughly ¼" outside the traced lines.

**2.** Following the manufacturer's instructions, press the fusible-web shapes onto the wrong sides of the designated fabrics; let cool. Cut out the fabric shapes on the drawn lines. Peel off the paper backing.

*From tan print, cut:*
- 12 of Pattern A
*From cranberry print, cut:*
- 5—1¼×51½" sashing strips
- 7—2½×42" binding strips
- 16—1¼×16½" sashing strips
- 48—1⅞" squares *or* 48 of Pattern B
- 12 of Pattern G
- 24 of Pattern H

*From dark blue print, cut:*
- 2—4½×68¼" border strips
- 2—4½×59½" border strips
- 24—2½×16½" strips
- 24—2½×12½" strips
- 48—2¼" squares, cutting each in half diagonally for a total of 96 triangles *or* 96 of Pattern C
*From mauve print, cut:*
- 24—4⅞"squares, cutting each in half diagonally for a total of 48 triangles *or* 96 of Pattern D
- 24 of Pattern G
- 12 of Pattern H
*From green print, cut:*
- 48 *each* of patterns E, F, and I
- 12 *each* of patterns J, J reversed, and K

## ASSEMBLE THE BLOCKS
**1.** Align one short edge of a dark blue print C triangle with one edge of a cranberry print B square. Sew together the pieces (see Diagram 1). Press the seam allowance toward the triangle. Add a second dark blue print C triangle to an adjacent side of the square to make an inside corner unit; press as before. Repeat to make a total of four inside corner units.

Diagram 1

# Promise of Spring

**4.** Sew an outside corner unit to one edge of the pieced square (see Diagram 4). Press the seam allowance toward the outside corner unit. Sew the remaining outside corner units to the remaining edges of the pieced square to make a pieced block. The pieced block should measure 12½" square, including the seam allowances.

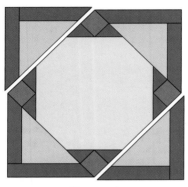

Diagram 4

**5.** Sew the dark blue print 2½×12½" strips to opposite edges of the pieced block. Then join the blue print 2½×16½" strips to the remaining edges of the pieced block. Press the seam allowances toward the dark blue print strips. The pieced block should measure 16½" square, including the seam allowances.

**6.** Repeat steps 1 through 5 to make a total of 12 pieced blocks.

**APPLIQUE THE BLOCKS**

**1.** To appliqué one block you'll need two mauve print G tulips, one cranberry print G tulip, two cranberry print H tulip tips, one mauve print H tulip tip, four green print I leaves, one green print K stem, one green print J curved

**2.** Sew an inside corner unit to a long edge of the tan print A piece as shown in Diagram 2. Press the seam allowance toward the tan piece. Add the remaining inside corner units to the remaining long edges of the tan piece to make a pieced square.

**3.** Referring to Diagram 3 for placement, join a green print E piece to one short edge of a mauve print D triangle. Press the seam allowance toward the green piece. Sew a green print F piece to the remaining short edge of the mauve print triangle to make an outside corner unit; press as before. Repeat to make a total of four outside corner units.

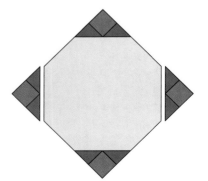

Diagram 2

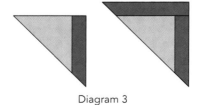

Diagram 3

stem, and one green print J reversed curved stem.

**2.** Referring to the photograph *opposite* for placement, arrange the appliqué pieces on a pieced block; fuse in place with a hot, dry iron.

**3.** Machine-blanket-stitch around the pieces with black sewing thread. If you'd prefer to hand-stitch the pieces in place, use two strands of black embroidery floss and the blanket stitch. (For instructions on the blanket stitch, see Appliqué Primer, which begins on *page 2.*)

**4.** Repeat steps 1 through 3 to applique the 12 pieced blocks.

## ASSEMBLE THE QUILT CENTER

**1.** Lay out the appliquéd tulip blocks in four horizontal rows of three blocks each, alternating the blocks with cranberry print 1¼×16½" sashing strips. Each row should begin and end with a sashing strip. Join the pieces in each row. Press the seam allowances in one direction. Each pieced row should measure 16½×51½", including the seam allowances.

**2.** Sew together the horizontal rows, alternating the rows with cranberry print 1¼×51½" sashing strips to complete the quilt center. The top and bottom rows should be sashing strips. Press as before. The pieced quilt center should measure 51½×68¼", including the seam allowances.

## ADD THE BORDERS

Sew the dark blue print 4½×68¼" border strips to the side edges of the pieced quilt center. Then add the dark blue print 4½×59½" border strips to the top and bottom edges of the pieced quilt center to complete the quilt top. Press all seam allowances toward the dark blue print border strips.

## COMPLETE THE QUILT

**1.** Layer the quilt top, batting and backing according to the instructions in Quilting Basics, which begins on *page 94.* Quilt as desired.

**2.** Use the cranberry print 2½×42" strips to bind the quilt according to the instructions in Quilting Basics.

## TULIP TIME

This version of "Promise of Spring" offers a cheery glow with charming yellow and pink pastels.

# Promise of Spring

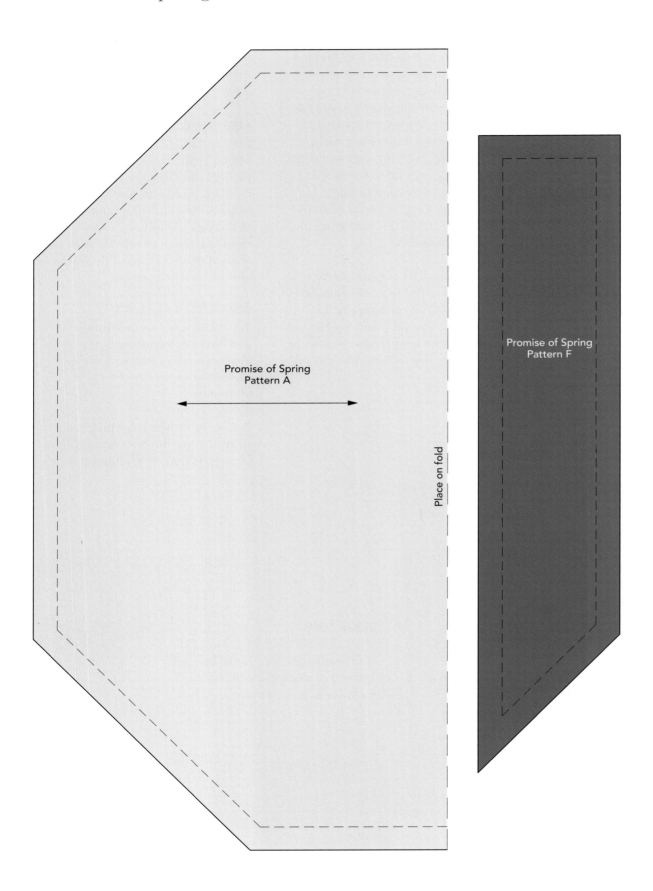

Promise of Spring
Pattern A

Place on fold

Promise of Spring
Pattern F

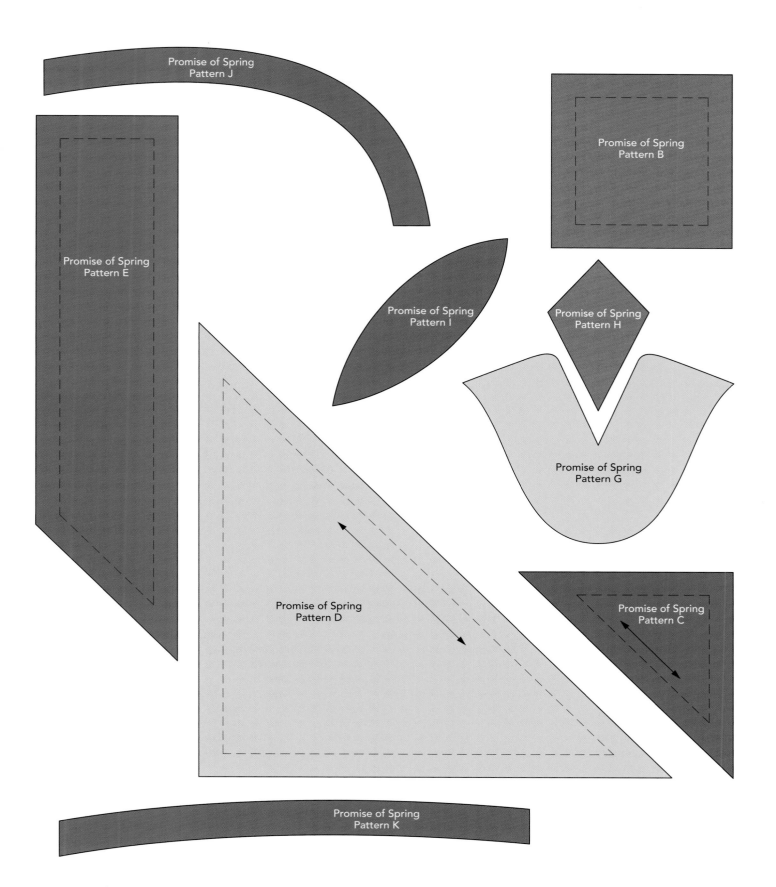

Promise of Spring
Pattern J

Promise of Spring
Pattern B

Promise of Spring
Pattern E

Promise of Spring
Pattern I

Promise of Spring
Pattern H

Promise of Spring
Pattern G

Promise of Spring
Pattern D

Promise of Spring
Pattern C

Promise of Spring
Pattern K

As patriotic as apple pie, this star-studded quilt is built upon a multitude of perfectly aligned Snowball blocks.

# Stars of Liberty

## MATERIALS

3 yards of dark blue print for blocks, borders, and binding
4⅜ yards of white floral for blocks and borders
1½ yards of solid red for star appliqués
5⅛ yards of backing fabric
71×92" of quilt batting
3 yards of lightweight fusible web

Finished quilt top: 65×86"
Finished block: 7" square

Quantities specified for 44/45"-wide, 100% cotton fabrics. All measurements include a ¼" seam allowance. Sew with right sides together unless otherwise stated.

Design: Teri Christopherson
Photographs: Scott Little;
    Marcia Cameron

## CUT THE FABRICS

To make the best use of your fabrics, cut the pieces in the order that follows. Cut the border strips lengthwise (parallel to the selvage). The Star Pattern is on *page 81*. To use fusible web for appliquéing, as was done in this project, complete the following steps.

**1.** Lay the fusible web, paper side up, over the pattern. Use a pencil to trace the pattern 54 times, leaving a ½" space between tracings. Cut out each piece roughly ¼" outside the traced lines.

**2.** Following the manufacturer's instructions, press the fusible-web shapes onto the wrong side of the solid red fabric; let cool. Cut out the fabric shapes on the drawn lines. Peel off the paper backing.

*From dark blue print, cut:*
- 8—2½×42" binding strips
- 2—1½×80½" border strips
- 2—1½×64½" border strips
- 2—1½×57½" border strips
- 2—1½×41½" border strips
- 20—7½" squares
- 80—3" squares

*From white floral, cut:*
- 2—7½×78½" border strips
- 2—7½×43½" border strips
- 2—3½×86" border strips
- 2—3½×62½" border strips
- 2—3½×59½" border strips
- 2—3½×35½" border strips
- 20—7½" squares
- 80—3" squares

*From solid red, cut:*
- 54 of Star Pattern

## ASSEMBLE THE SNOWBALL BLOCKS

**1.** For accurate sewing lines, use a quilter's pencil to mark a diagonal line on the wrong side of the white floral 3" squares. (To prevent your fabric from stretching as you draw the lines, place 220-grit sandpaper under the squares.)

**2.** Align a marked white floral 3" square with each corner of a dark blue print 7½" square (see the Block Assembly Diagram; note the placement of the diagonal lines). Stitch on the marked sewing lines; trim the seam allowances to ¼". Press the attached triangles open to make a Snowball block. The pieced block should still measure 7½" square, including the seam allowances.

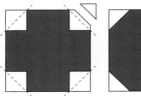

Block Assembly Diagram

**3.** Repeat Step 2 to make a total of 20 dark blue Snowball blocks.

# Stars of Liberty

**2.** Sew together the blocks in each row. Press the seam allowances toward the dark blue Snowball blocks. Then join the rows to complete the quilt center. Press the seam allowances in one direction. The pieced quilt center should measure 35½×56½", including the seam allowances.

## ADD THE BORDER

**1.** Sew the white floral 3½×35½" border strips to the short edges of the pieced quilt center. Then add the white floral 3½×62½" border strips to the long edges of the pieced quilt center. Press the seam allowances toward the white floral border.

**2.** Sew the dark blue print 1½×41½" border strips to the short edges of the pieced quilt center. Then add the dark blue print 1½×64½" border strips to the long edges of the pieced quilt center. Press the seam allowances toward the dark blue print border.

**3.** Sew the white floral 7½×43½" border strips to the short edges of the pieced quilt center. Then add the white floral 7½×78½" border strips to the long edges of the pieced quilt center. Press the seam allowances toward the white floral border.

**4.** Repeat steps 1 and 2 using dark blue print 3" squares and white floral 7½" squares to make a total of 20 blue Snowball blocks.

**5.** Referring to the photograph *above* for placement, position a solid red star appliqué in the center of each blue Snowball block; fuse in place.

**6.** Using thread in a color that matches the fabric, machine-blanket-stitch the appliqués in place.

## ASSEMBLE THE QUILT CENTER

**1.** Referring to the photograph *above*, lay out the 20 dark blue Snowball blocks and the 20 appliquéd Snowball blocks in eight horizontal rows, alternating the blocks.

**4.** Referring to the photograph *above left* for placement, position the remaining 34 solid red star appliqués on the 7½"-wide white floral border. When pleased with the placement, fuse in place.

**5.** Using thread in a color that matches the fabric, machine-blanket-stitch the appliqués in place.

**6.** Sew the dark blue print 1½×57½" border strips to the short edges of the pieced quilt center. Then add the dark blue print 1½×80½" border strips to the long edges of the pieced quilt center. Press the seam allowances toward the dark blue print border.

**7.** Sew the white floral 3½×59½" border strips to the short edges of the pieced quilt center. Then add the white floral 3½×86½" border strips to the long edges of the pieced quilt center to complete the quilt top. Press the seam allowances toward the white floral border.

### COMPLETE THE QUILT

**1.** Layer the quilt top, batting, and backing according to the instructions in Quilting Basics, which begins on *page 94.* Quilt as desired.

**2.** Use the dark blue print 2½×42" strips to bind the quilt according to the instructions in Quilting Basics.

Stars of Liberty
Star Pattern

### PATRIOTIC SALUTE

Stay with the Fourth of July theme, but choose brick red, colonial blue, and warm gold to complement an old-fashioned conversation print.

In holiday colors, this Cherry Wreath block ushers in the holidays—and extends them gracefully into the New Year.

# Cherry Wreath

## MATERIALS

⅜ yard of cream print for appliqué foundations
½ yard of green print for leaf appliqués, sashing strips, inner border, and corner squares
⅓ yard of red print for cherry appliqués and outer border
⅔ yard of backing fabric
22×45" of quilt batting
¾ yard of lightweight fusible web

Finished quilt top: 16½×39½"
Finished block: 10½" square

Quantities specified for 44/45"-wide, 100% cotton fabrics. All measurements include a ¼" seam allowance. Sew with right sides together unless otherwise stated.

Design: Peggy Kotek
Photographs: Scott Little;
    Marcia Cameron

## CUT THE FABRICS

To make the best use of your fabrics, cut the pieces in the order that follows. The patterns are on *page 84*. To use fusible web for appliquéing, as was done in this project, complete the following steps.

**1.** Lay the fusible web, paper side up, over the patterns. Use a pencil to trace each pattern the number of times indicated, leaving a ½" space between tracings. Cut out each piece roughly ¼" outside the traced lines.

**2.** Following the manufacturer's instructions, press the fusible-web shapes onto the wrong sides of the designated fabrics; let cool. Cut out the fabric shapes on the drawn lines. Peel off the paper backing.

*From cream print, cut:*
- 3—11" squares for appliqué foundations

*From green print, cut:*
- 2—1½×34" inner border strips
- 2—1½×13" inner border strips
- 2—1½×11" sashing strips
- 4—2½" border corner squares
- 3 of Pattern A
- 45 of Pattern B
- 12 of Pattern C

*From red print, cut:*
- 2—2½×36" outer border strips
- 2—2½×13" outer border strips
- 45 of Pattern D

*From backing fabric, cut:*
- 1—24×42" piece

## APPLIQUÉ THE CHERRY WREATH BLOCK

**1.** Referring to the Appliqué Placement Diagram, arrange a green print A ring, 15 green print B leaves, four green print C stems, and 15 red print D cherries on a cream print 11" foundation square; fuse in place.

Appliqué Placement Diagram

**2.** Use coordinating thread to machine-blanket-stitch the appliqués in place to make a Cherry Wreath block.

**3.** Repeat steps 1 and 2 to make a total of three Cherry Wreath blocks.

# Cherry Wreath

## ASSEMBLE THE QUILT CENTER

**1.** Referring to the photograph on *page 83* for placement, lay out the three appliquéd blocks and the two green print 1½×11" sashing strips in a row.

**2.** Sew together the pieces to make the quilt center. Press the seam allowances toward the sashing strips.

## ADD THE BORDERS

**1.** Sew the green print 1½×34" inner border strips to the long edges of the pieced quilt center. Then add the green print 1½×13" inner border strips to the short edges of the pieced quilt center. Press the seam allowances toward the inner border.

**2.** Sew the red print 2½×36" outer border strips to the long edges of the pieced quilt center. Press the seam allowances toward the outer border. Sew a green print 2½" corner square to each end of the red print 2½×13" outer border strips. Press the seam allowances toward the green print squares. Then add the pieced outer border strips to the short edges of the pieced quilt center to complete the quilt top.

Press the seam allowances toward the outer border.

## COMPLETE THE QUILT

**1.** Layer the quilt batting, backing, and then the quilt top with right sides together. Stitch around the unit with a ¼" seam allowance, leaving a 3" opening for turning.

**2.** Trim the backing to a ¼" seam allowance. Trim the quilt batting up to the stitching. Turn the unit right side out. Slip-stitch the opening closed. Quilt as desired.

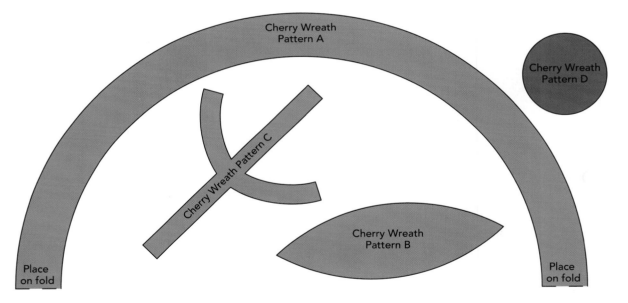

## DRESS IT UP

The gold inner border and green outer border give this variation a dressier finished look.

# Field of Flowers Sweatshirt

Warm a chill with a cozy sunflower sweatshirt.
Square blocks, already appliquéd, are a cinch to
sew on an unwieldy sweatshirt.

**MATERIALS FOR SWEATSHIRT**

Pre-washed pigment-dyed sweatshirt
⅛ yard of solid black for block
    foundations
9" square of blue print for sky
    appliqués
9" square of green print for stem and
    leaf appliqués
9" square of yellow print for flower
    petal appliqués
Scrap of rust print for flower center
    appliqués
¼ yard of lightweight fusible web
No. 5 black perle cotton thread
Basting spray (optional)

Finished block: 4×5¾"

Quantities specified for 44/45"-wide,
100% cotton fabrics.

Design: Kathleen Parman
Photographs: Perry Struse;
    Marcia Cameron

**CUT THE FABRICS**

To make the best use of your fabrics,
cut the pieces in the order that
follows. The patterns are on *page 87*.
To use fusible web for appliquéing,
as was done in this project, complete
the following steps.

# Field of Flowers Sweatshirt

**1.** Lay the fusible web, paper side up, over the patterns. Use a pencil, to trace each pattern the number of times indicated, leaving a ½" space between tracings. Cut out each piece roughly ¼" outside the traced lines.

**2.** Following the manufacturer's instructions, press the fusible-web shapes onto the wrong sides of the designated fabrics; let cool. Cut out the fabric shapes on the drawn lines. Peel off the paper backing.

*From solid black, cut:*
- 3—4×5¾" rectangles
*From blue print, cut:*
- 3 *each* of patterns A through F
*From green print, cut:*
- 3 of Pattern G
*From yellow print, cut:*
- 3 *each* of patterns H through Q
*From rust print, cut:*
- 3 of Pattern R

## PRACTICE THE TECHNIQUE

Thread your machine, both top and bobbin, with black thread. Attach a free-motion quilting or darning foot to your machine and drop the feed dogs. (*Note:* If your machine doesn't have this feature, tape a business card over the feed dogs to prevent them from "grabbing" the fabric.)

Practice a machine-stitching technique designer Kathleen Parman calls "herky-jerky stitching" on fabric scraps. This modified free-motion stipple quilting uses small, uneven stitches that cross over previous stitches to attach the appliqué pieces to the foundations and the foundations to the sweatshirt (see detail photograph at *right*).

Begin practicing this technique with a few extra appliqué pieces fused to a practice block. Position your block under the presser foot and manually lower the needle down through the edge of an appliqué piece and back up along the same edge. Using the top thread, pull up the bobbin thread so both threads are coming through the top side of the appliqué.

While holding the threads to secure them, start making small stitches in uneven circular and triangular motions. You should be stitching in a relatively steady rhythm as you move the scrap around so that you stitch on and off the appliqué edges and onto the foundation scrap.

## APPLIQUÉ THE SWEATSHIRT

**1.** Referring to the Appliqué Placement Diagram, arrange the appliqué pieces on the solid black 4×5¾" rectangles, leaving approximately ¼" between pieces. Fuse the lower sky and stem pieces to the black rectangles first. Adjust the position of the flower pieces as

necessary, then fuse the flowers in place to make a total of three flower blocks.

Appliqué Placement Diagram

**2.** Center a flower block on the sweatshirt; baste in place with basting spray or basting stitches. Try on the sweatshirt to confirm the block's position. Using the herky-jerky technique, stitch around all of the appliqués' edges, stitching from one appliqué piece to the next without stopping to cut threads. Stitch the outer edges of the flower block to the sweatshirt in the same manner. Repeat the stitching with the remaining two flower blocks.

**3.** To finish the sweatshirt, cut off its bottom ribbing and turn up a ½" hem to the outside. Use black perle cotton thread to stitch the turned-up hem with a ½" running stitch. Fold the neckline ribbing in half, turning it toward the right side. Use black perle cotton thread to stitch the turned-down ribbing with a ¼" running stitch.

Field of Flowers Sweatshirt
Full-Size Patterns

## COOL BREEZES

For a lighter look, opt for medium blue foundations and thread, plus daisies in three different colors on a bright white T-shirt.

The contrast between a tone-on-tone print and a geometric check outlines the paths for groups of flowers.

# A Walk in the Garden

## MATERIALS

2¾ yards of light tan stripe for appliqué foundations, alternate blocks, inner border, and pieced border

2½ yards of tan check for appliqué foundations, alternate blocks, and pieced border

¼ yard of dark red print for pieced border

¼ yard of dark green print No. 1 for pieced border

1½ yards of dark green polka dot for outer border

¾ yard of dark green print No. 2 for binding

1½ yards total of assorted red, green, purple, and gold prints for flower appliqués

5⅓ yards of backing fabric

74×94" of quilt batting

3 yards of lightweight fusible web

Black machine-embroidery thread

Finished block: 10" square
Finished quilt top: 67½×87½"

Quantities specified for 44/45"-wide, 100% cotton fabrics. All measurements include a ¼" seam allowance. Sew with right sides together unless otherwise stated.

Design: Barb Anna and Deb Crnkovich
Photographs: Perry Struse;
　　Steve Struse

## CUT THE FABRICS

To make the best use of your fabrics, cut the pieces in the order that follows. The patterns are on *pages 92 and 93*. To use fusible web for appliquéing, as was done in this project, complete the following steps.

**1.** Lay the fusible web, paper side up, over the patterns. Use a pencil to trace each pattern the number of times indicated, leaving a ½" space between tracings. Cut out each piece roughly ¼" outside the traced lines.

**2.** Following the manufacturer's instructions, press the fusible-web shapes onto the wrong side of the designated fabrics; let cool. Cut out the fabric shapes on the drawn lines. Peel off the paper backing.

*From light tan stripe, cut:*
- 2—3×42" strips for pieced border
- 7—1¾×42" strips for inner border
- 9—12½" squares for appliqué foundations
- 9—10⅞" squares, cutting each in half diagonally to make a total of 18 triangles for alternate blocks

*From tan check, cut:*
- 2—3×42" strips for pieced border
- 8—12½" squares for appliqué foundations

- 9—10⅞" squares, cutting each in half diagonally to make a total of 18 triangles for alternate blocks
- 2—3" squares for pieced border

*From dark red print, cut:*
- 2—3×42" strips for pieced border

*From dark green print No. 1, cut:*
- 2—3×42" strips for pieced border

*From dark green polka dot, cut:*
- 8—5½×42" strips for outer border

*From dark green print No. 2, cut:*
- 8—2¾×42" binding strips

*From assorted red prints, cut:*
- 2 of Pattern A
- 8 of Pattern G
- 5 of Pattern K
- 4 *each* of patterns N and O
- 6 of Pattern T

*From assorted green prints, cut:*
- 2 *each* of patterns D, E, E reversed, U, V, and V reversed
- 4 *each* of patterns H, I, I reversed, Q, R, and R reversed
- 5 each of patterns L and M

*From assorted purple fabrics, cut:*
- 12 of Pattern G
- 6 of Pattern T

*From assorted gold prints, cut:*
- 2 *each* of patterns B, B reversed, C, and S
- 4 *each* of patterns F and P
- 5 of Pattern J

# A Walk in the Garden

## APPLIQUÉ THE FLOWER BLOCKS

**1.** Place the fused appliqué shapes for flowers No. 1, 3, and 5 on the light tan stripe appliqué foundation squares (refer to the photograph at *left* and assembly diagrams *below* for placement). Place the fused appliqué shapes for flowers No. 2 and 4 on the tan check appliqué foundation squares. Overlap the appliqué shapes as needed. Fuse the pieces in place.

**2.** Using the black machine-embroidery thread, machine-blanket-stitch around each fused piece.

**3.** Trim each appliquéd flower block to 10½" square, including the seam allowances.

## ASSEMBLE THE TRIANGLE-SQUARES

**1.** Referring to Diagram 1 for placement, sew together one light tan stripe triangle and one tan check triangle to make a triangle-square. Press the seam allowance toward the tan check triangle. The pieced triangle-square should measure 10½" square, including the seam allowances.

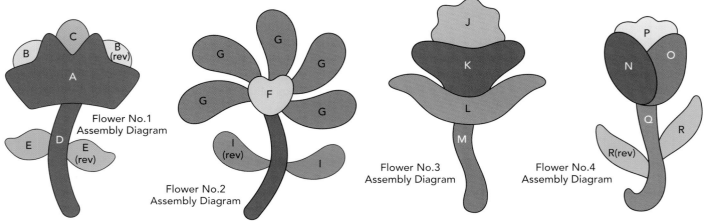

Flower No.1
Assembly Diagram

Flower No.2
Assembly Diagram

Flower No.3
Assembly Diagram

Flower No.4
Assembly Diagram

Diagram 1

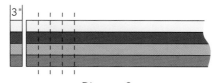

Diagram 3

Diagram 4

**2.** Repeat to make a total of 18 triangle-squares.

## ASSEMBLE THE QUILT CENTER

**1.** Referring to the photograph *opposite* for placement, lay out the flower blocks and triangle-squares in seven horizontal rows of five squares each. Sew together the squares in each row. Press the seam allowances toward the flower blocks.

**2.** Then join the rows to make the quilt center. Press the seam allowances in one direction. The pieced quilt center should measure 50½×70½", including the seam allowances.

## ADD THE INNER BORDER

**1.** Cut and piece the light tan stripe 1¾×42" strips to make the following:
- 2—1¾×73" inner border strips
- 2—1¾×50½" inner border strips

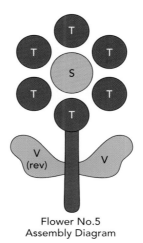

Flower No.5
Assembly Diagram

**2.** Sew the short light tan stripe inner border strips to the top and bottom edges of the pieced quilt center. Then add the long light tan stripe inner border strips to the side edges of the pieced quilt center. Press the seam allowances toward the light tan stripe border.

## ASSEMBLE AND ADD THE PIECED BORDER

**1.** Referring to Diagram 2 for placement, sew together a dark green print No. 1, tan check, dark red print, and light tan stripe 3×42" strip to make a strip set. Press the seam allowances in one direction. Repeat to make a second strip set. Cut the two strip sets into a total of twenty-six 3"-wide segments.

Diagram 2

**2.** Referring to Diagram 3 for placement, sew together five 3"-wide segments and one tan check 3" square to make a pieced border strip. Press the seam allowances in one direction. Repeat to make a second pieced border strip. Sew the pieced border strips to the top and bottom edges of the pieced quilt center. Press the seam allowances toward the light tan inner border.

**3.** Referring to Diagram 4 for placement, sew together eight

3"-wide segments to make a pieced side border strip. Remove one green print square from one end of the pieced side border strip. Press the seam allowances in one direction. Repeat to make a second pieced side border strip. Sew the pieced side border strips to the side edges of the quilt center. Press the seam allowances toward the light tan inner border. The pieced quilt center should measure 58×78", including the seam allowances.

## ADD THE OUTER BORDER

**1.** Cut and piece the dark green polka-dot 5½×42" strips to make the following:
- 2—5½×88" outer border strips
- 2—5½×58" outer border strips

**2.** Sew the short dark green polka-dot outer border strips to the top and bottom edges of the pieced quilt center. Then add the long dark green polka-dot outer border strips to the side edges of the pieced quilt center to complete the quilt top. Press all seam allowances toward the dark green polka-dot border.

## COMPLETE THE QUILT TOP

**1.** Layer the quilt top, batting, and backing according to the instructions in Quilting Basics, which begins on *page 94*. Quilt as desired.

**2.** Use the dark green print 2¾×42" strips to bind the quilt according to the instructions in Quilting Basics.

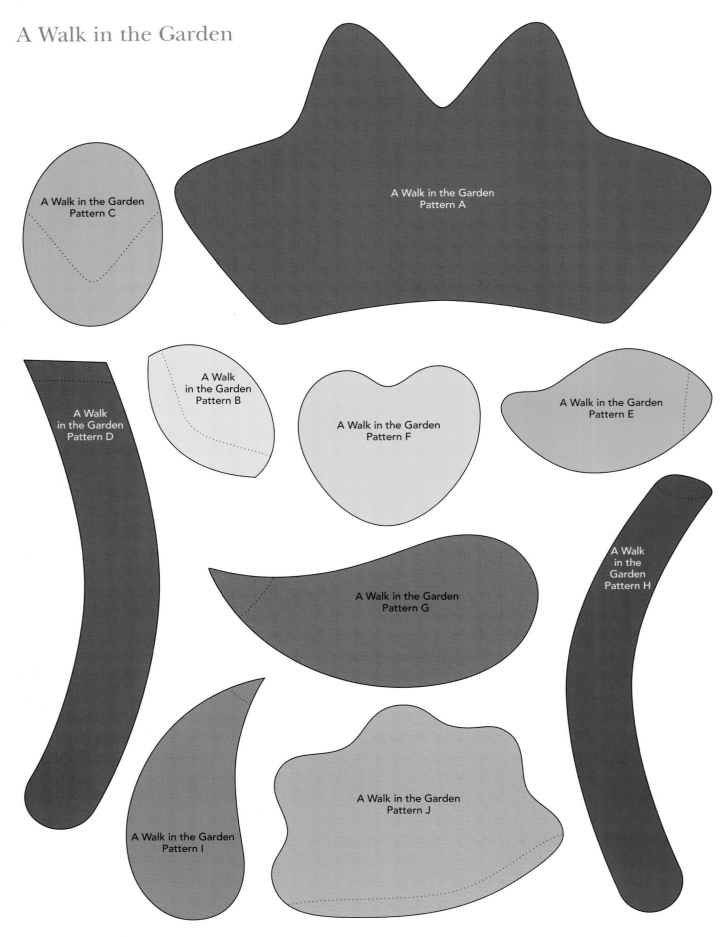

A Walk in the Garden
Pattern C

A Walk in the Garden
Pattern A

A Walk
in the Garden
Pattern D

A Walk
in the Garden
Pattern B

A Walk in the Garden
Pattern F

A Walk in the Garden
Pattern E

A Walk
in the
Garden
Pattern H

A Walk in the Garden
Pattern G

A Walk in the Garden
Pattern I

A Walk in the Garden
Pattern J

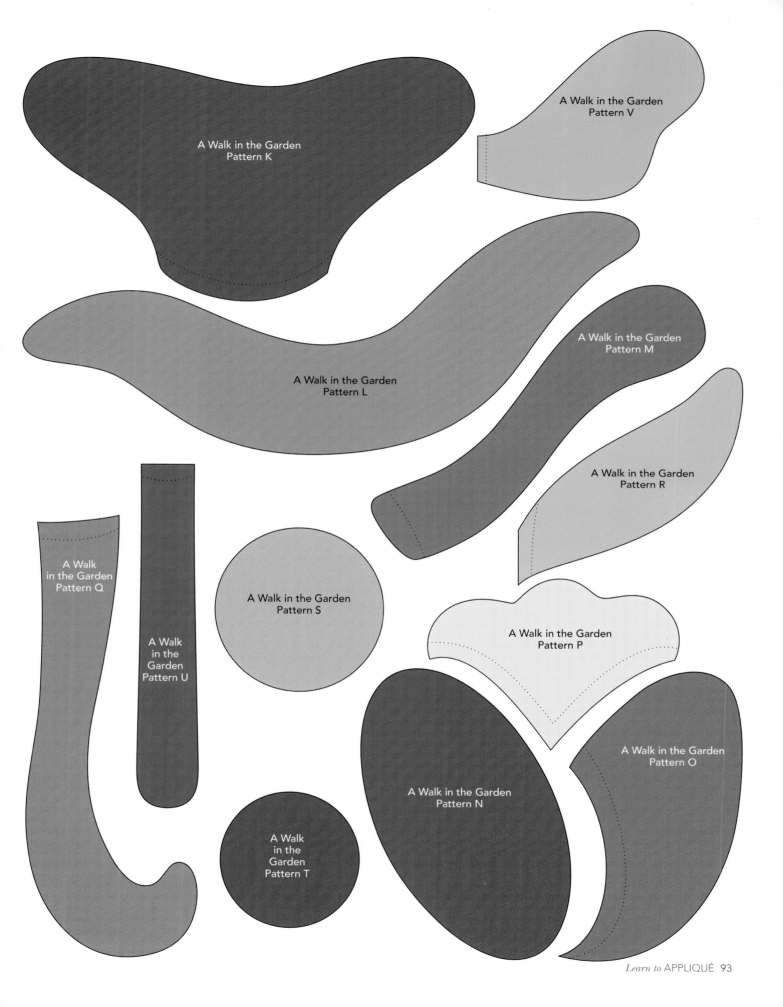

A Walk in the Garden
Pattern K

A Walk in the Garden
Pattern V

A Walk in the Garden
Pattern L

A Walk in the Garden
Pattern M

A Walk in the Garden
Pattern R

A Walk
in the Garden
Pattern Q

A Walk
in the
Garden
Pattern U

A Walk in the Garden
Pattern S

A Walk in the Garden
Pattern P

A Walk in the Garden
Pattern O

A Walk
in the
Garden
Pattern T

A Walk in the Garden
Pattern N

# Quilting Basics

Read through these general quilting instructions to ensure you'll properly cut and assemble your quilt. Accuracy in each step guarantees a successful quiltmaking experience.

## *Getting Started*

### TOOLS
#### BASIC
**Acrylic ruler:** To aid in making perfectly straight cuts with a rotary cutter, choose a ruler of thick, clear plastic. Many sizes are available. A 6×24" ruler marked in ¼" increments with 30°, 45°, and 60° angles is a good first purchase.

**Rotary-cutting mat:** A rotary cutter should always be used with a mat designed specifically for it. In addition to protecting the table, the mat helps keep the fabric from shifting while you cut. Often these mats are described as self-healing, meaning the blade does not leave slash marks or grooves in the surface, even after repeated usage.

**Rotary cutter:** The round blade of a rotary cutter will cut up to six layers of fabric at once. Because the blade is so sharp, be sure to purchase one with a safety guard and keep the guard over the blade when you're not cutting. The blade can be removed from the handle and replaced when it gets dull.

**Scissors:** You'll need one pair for cutting fabric and another for cutting paper and plastic.

**Pencils and other marking tools:** Marks made with special quilt markers are easy to remove after sewing.

**Template plastic:** This slightly frosted plastic comes in sheets about ¹⁄₁₆" thick.

**Iron and ironing board:** Pressing the seams ensures accurate piecing.

**Sewing thread:** Use 100% cotton thread.

**Sewing machine:** Any machine in good working order with well-adjusted tension will produce pucker-free patchwork seams.

### HAND QUILTING
**Frame or hoop:** You'll get smaller, more even stitches if you stretch your quilt as you stitch. A frame supports the quilt's weight, ensures even tension, and frees both your hands for stitching. However, once set up, it cannot be disassembled until the quilting is complete. Quilting hoops are more portable and less expensive.

**Quilting needles:** A "between" or quilting needle is short with a small eye. Common sizes are 8, 9, and 10; size 8 is best for beginners.

**Quilting thread:** Quilting thread is stronger than sewing thread.

**Thimble:** This finger cover relieves the pressure required to push a needle through several layers of fabric and batting.

### MACHINE QUILTING
**Darning foot:** You may find this tool, also called a hopper foot, in your sewing machine's accessory kit. If not, have the model and brand of your machine available when you go to purchase one. It is used for free-motion stitching.

**Safety pins:** They hold the layers together during quilting.

**Table:** Use a large work surface that's level with your machine bed.

**Thread:** Use 100% cotton quilting thread, cotton-wrapped polyester quilting thread, or fine nylon monofilament thread.

**Walking foot:** This sewing-machine accessory helps you keep long, straight quilting lines smooth and pucker-free.

### CHOOSE YOUR FABRICS
It is no surprise that most quilters prefer 100% cotton fabrics for quiltmaking. Cotton fabric minimizes seam distortion, presses crisply, and is easy to quilt. Most patterns, including those in this book, specify quantities for 44/45"-wide fabrics unless otherwise noted. Our projects call for a little extra yardage in length to allow for minor errors and slight shrinkage.

### PREPARE YOUR FABRICS
There are conflicting opinions about the need to prewash fabric. The debate is a modern one because most antique quilts were made with unwashed fabric. However, the dyes and sizing used today are unlike those used a century ago.

Prewashing fabric offers quilters certainty as its main advantage. Today's fabrics resist bleeding and shrinkage, but some of both can occur in some fabrics—an unpleasant prospect once you've assembled a quilt. Some quilters find prewashed fabric easier to quilt. If you choose to prewash your fabric, press it well before cutting.

Other quilters prefer the crispness of unwashed fabric, especially for machine piecing. And, if you use fabrics with the same fiber content throughout a quilt, then any shrinkage that occurs in its first washing should be uniform. Some quilters find this small amount of shrinkage desirable, since it gives a quilt a slightly puckered, antique look.

We recommend you prewash a scrap of each fabric to test it for shrinkage and bleeding. If you choose to prewash an entire fabric piece, unfold it to a single layer. Wash it in warm water, which will allow the fabric to shrink and/or bleed. If the fabric bleeds, rinse it until the water runs clear. Do not use it in a quilt if it hasn't stopped bleeding. Hang the fabric to dry, or tumble it in the dryer until slightly damp; press well.

# Finishing

## LAYERING

Cut and piece the backing fabric to measure at least 3" bigger on all sides than the quilt top. Press all seam allowances open. With wrong sides together, layer the quilt top and backing fabric with the batting in between; baste. Quilt as desired.

## BINDING

The binding for most quilts is cut on the straight grain of the fabric. If your quilt has curved edges, cut the strips on the bias (see Appliqué Primer, which begins on *page 2*). The cutting instructions for projects in this book specify the number of

binding strips or a total length needed to finish the quilt. The instructions also specify enough width for a French-fold, or double-layer, binding because it's easier to apply and adds durability.

Join the strips with diagonal seams to make one continuous binding strip (see Diagram 1). Trim the excess fabric, leaving ¼" seam allowances. Press seam allowances open. Then, with the wrong sides together, fold under 1" at one end of the binding strip (see Diagram 2); press. Fold the strip in half lengthwise (see Diagram 3); press.

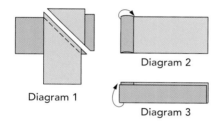

Diagram 1

Diagram 2

Diagram 3

Beginning in the center of one side, place the binding strip against the right side of the quilt top, aligning the binding strip's raw edges with the quilt top's raw edge (see Diagram 4). Beginning 1½" from the folded edge, sew through all layers, stopping ¼" from the corner. Backstitch, then clip the threads. Remove the quilt from under the sewing-machine presser foot.

Fold the binding strip upward (see Diagram 5), creating a diagonal fold, and finger-press.

Holding the diagonal fold in place with your finger, bring the binding strip down in line with the next edge, making a horizontal fold that aligns with the first edge of the quilt (see Diagram 6).

Start sewing again at the top of the horizontal fold, stitching through all

layers. Sew around the quilt, turning each corner in the same manner.

When you return to the starting point, lap the binding strip inside the beginning fold (see Diagram 7). Finish sewing to the starting point (see Diagram 8). Trim the batting and backing fabric even with the quilt top edges.

Turn the binding over the edge of the quilt to the back. Hand-stitch the binding to the backing fabric, making sure to cover any machine stitching.

To make mitered corners on the back, hand-stitch the binding up to a corner; fold a miter in the binding. Take a stitch or two in the fold to secure it. Then stitch the binding in place up to the next corner. Finish each corner in the same manner.

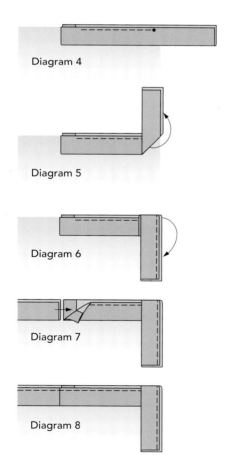

Diagram 4

Diagram 5

Diagram 6

Diagram 7

Diagram 8

# Better Homes and Gardens®
# Creative Collection™

**Editorial Director**
Gayle Goodson Butler

**Editor-in-Chief**
Beverly Rivers

**Executive Editor**   Karman Wittry Hotchkiss

**Editorial Manager**   **Art Director**
Ann Blevins   Brenda Drake Lesch

### American Patchwork & Quilting®

**Executive Editor**   Heidi Kaisand
**Art Director**   Melissa Gansen Beauchamp
**Contributing Graphic Designer**   Barbara J. Gordon

**Copy Chief**   Mary Heaton
**Contributing Copy Editor**   Lisa Flyr
**Contributing Proofreader**   Joleen Ross
**Administrative Assistant**   Lori Eggers

**Senior Vice President**
Bob Mate

**Vice President, Publishing Director**
William R. Reed

**Group Publisher**   Stephen B. Levinson
**Group Marketing Director**   Cathy E. Smith
**General Manager**   Tom Harty
**Senior Marketing Manager**   Suzy Johnson

**Publishing Group President**
Jack Griffin

# Meredith
CORPORATION

**Chairman and CEO**   William T. Kerr
**President and COO**   Stephen M. Lacy

**In Memoriam**
E. T. Meredith III (1933–2003)